Great Meetings Build Great Teams

Great Meetings Build Great Teams

A Guide for Project Leaders and Agilists

Rich Maltzman, PMP® and Jim Stewart, PMP®

BEP

BUSINESS EXPERT PRESS

Leader in applied, concise business books

Description

Want happier, more successful project teams? Better-run meetings will help get you there. Project leaders are *get it done* people, so we often dislike, avoid, and/or fail to properly plan meetings. This practical guide to facilitating project meetings and building cohesive teams will enable you to make your sessions more productive!

You'll learn:

- How improving traditional PM meetings and Agile events can greatly improve continuous team building, making you a better project leader
- Overcoming challenges in managing conflict based on real-world stories from your fellow project leaders
- How to deal with *goblins* (e.g., Billy the Bully) who often derail your meetings

Aligned with PMI's *PMBOK® Guide Seventh Edition*, this book will help you deliver project success in today's hybrid work environment.

Keywords

meetings; teams; facilitation; project management; project communications; conflict management; remote work

Contents

Foreword

In my role as the head of a global PMO (Project Management Office), with team members in five countries round the world, we settled on a tagline for our group, which is "Together Everyone Achieves More" (TEAM), and we truly believe this to be true.

At the heart of being together is the way that we communicate with each other in an open, honest, sharing, challenging, questioning, supporting, and achieving way, together with a good dose of fun. Of course, anyone who has worked for me or attended one of my presentations will know that this is an absolute must.

Meetings, in the broadest sense, happen all the time. Every day. Planned, unplanned, full-team, part-team, with me, without me, every mix you can think of, and they provide a platform for information exchange, decision making, social interaction, and much more.

They should never be bottlenecks or ways to delay progress or simply fill time, and they should always have a clear purpose, together with my personal mantra, that they should never be any longer than they need to be.

And of course, today they will be a mixture of remote and physical. We live in a hybrid world.

So, what does all this mean for the project leader?

Consider the typical aspects of such leadership:

- Communication skills
- Interpersonal skills
- Teamwork skills
- Motivational skills
- Analytical skills
- Problem-solving skills
- Decision-making skills, and
- Conflict resolution

... all of these come to play in the project meeting environment.

Meetings, and the opportunity to interact with your team members and understand their current personal sentiment, are critical to being able to build and lead a high-performing team. We all know that projects are, and always have been, about people.

If I consider project success, in my world and almost certainly in your world as well, then success is a combination of experience and outcome. And to be truly successful, both need to be delivered by a project team. A good outcome through a bad experience of change leaves a lingering after-effect, but naturally, a good experience that delivers a bad outcome (if that is even possible) is not a positive end result either.

The *new* concept of project management as a system of value delivery (I personally think this has been the case for a long time, but it is being spoken of a great deal these days and is included in the Seventh Edition of PMI's *A Guide to the Project Management Body of Knowledge (PMBOK® Guide)* speaks to demanding a coordinated focus on all project activity and all such activity delivery planned for business outcomes, with the assumption of a low disruptive project experience.

But wait a minute, aren't projects by nature disruptive and, project managers aside, aren't most people uncomfortable during this period, longing only for the end of the project and the stability of a good outcome?

Of course they are. But communication calms this fear, and good communication comes from the right information, provided at the right time, to the right person, and in the right way.

Meetings, good meetings, can tick all four of these boxes and really deliver to everyone involved. But and this is one very big but, not everyone likes meetings, or thinks that they offer value for time, or indeed that the meetings they *do* attend are always well structured or deliver the necessary outcomes, but everyone I know believes that good meetings contribute to building great teams.

And, as such, we could all do with a little help; therefore, you might consider the following breakdown of need for such insights, which will guide your investment decision-making process a little more in this whole 'meetings and project teams' area.

Wherever you show up in Figure F.1, I commend to you this book *Great Meetings Build Great Teams: A Guide for Project Leaders and Agilists*

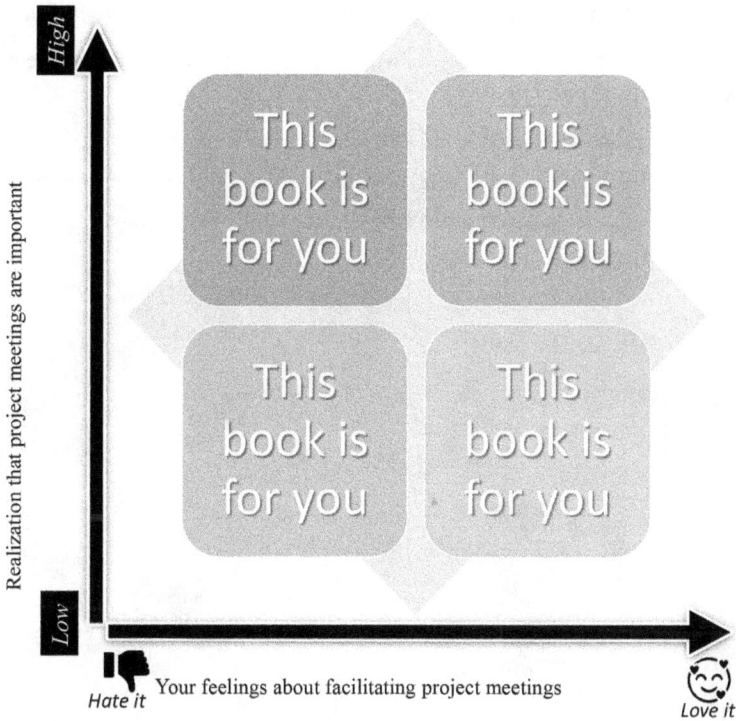

Figure F.1 This book is for you

to aid your safe navigation of the world of projects and project teams, which have a special dynamic about them, but which also deliver some truly amazing results around the world.

Thank you to my fantastic Global PMO team at Ceridian, together, we truly do achieve more.

I'm off to a meeting now, and I am looking forward to it.

—Peter Taylor

Author of *The Lazy Project Manager* and

Head of Global PMO for Ceridian

Peter Taylor is also a keynote speaker and coach and the author of the number one bestselling project management book *The Lazy Project Manager*, along with many other books on project management, PMO development, executive sponsorship, transformation leadership, and speaking skills.

He has built and led some of the largest PMOs in the world, with organizations such as Siemens, IBM, UKG, and now Ceridian, where he is the VP Global PMO.

He has also delivered over 450 lectures around the world in over 25 countries and has been described as "perhaps the most entertaining and inspiring speaker in the project management world today."

www.thelazyprojectmanager.com

Preface

The key to creating real and sustainable change in an organization is communicating with purpose. Your goal is to use every interaction and method of communication to drive actions and decisions. Every report you create, every meeting you have, everything that you do should be enabling the outcomes the organization is trying to achieve. If they aren't, why are you there?

—Laura Barnard 2021 World PMO Influencer of the Year
Chief IMPACT Driver, PMO Strategies
President, PM4Change (nonprofit)

Greetings from Jim Stewart, PMP, and Rich Maltzman, PMP. We wrote this book because we both firmly believe that while running great meetings isn't the only ingredient you need to make your projects successful, running poor meetings is a recipe for sending even the best project headlong toward failure.

Yes, we know—you already have too many meetings, and they are often back-to-back. And when you're not in the meeting—or perhaps even *during* the meeting—you are catching up on the 200+ e-mails you get per day.

Did you ever stop and ask yourself the following question? Is this normal? (Well, the meeting thing anyway. The e-mail thing could fill another separate book.)

And another thing—why *are* there so many meetings? Why is it that as the day goes on, each meeting runs over a little bit so that your final one is like the last plane out of LaGuardia Airport—very late and possibly even canceled.

We think that the real question is not "why are there so many meetings?" The question we ask is "why are meetings run so poorly, and so ineffectively that nothing on the agenda is covered?" Uh … you do *have* an agenda, right?

In this book, we endeavor to share with you our collective years of running projects, meetings and—often—our mouths. You'll learn tips, tricks and, we assert, a more effective way to run a meeting. You say you want to be creative? Then take up macrame. Because if we have to drive over bridges, we want to drive over bridges that are built according to sound project management best practices, which includes running productive meetings.

Meetings are (or should be) straightforward sessions that (1) have an agenda; (2) progress through that agenda; (3) accomplish their objectives, and (4) send attendees off more informed, engaged, and energized with clear direction. But hold on, don't completely abandon creativity—there are some things you can do to keep your attendees present and focused. We'll share those ideas with you, too.

Before we get into all that stuff, we thought you might like to hear how Steve Jobs approached meetings. He was famous for taking long walks while he was meeting. But regardless of whether it was in a conference room or in walk down a long hallway, Jobs had certain criteria that he preferred:

1. **Invite only a few people, no more than five.**
   The more people, the less productive. Therefore, less gets accomplished. So, less is more. Keep the invite list small—ideally, three to five people. (The authors would argue that kickoff and other such meetings require a larger quorum. But we get where Jobs is going.)
2. **Have an agenda but keep it to only a few items**.
   Focus, focus, focus.
3. **Keep it short—no more than 30 minutes**
   As we mentioned, people have a million meetings. And it's hard for people to stay focused when it goes longer. If you schedule it for 30 minutes and actually get it done in 15, that's a bonus! Senior management especially will love you. There's nothing people like to hear you say more than "I can put 10 minutes (or whatever) back in your day."

Lastly, there's always the question of—*is this meeting really necessary?* One manager used to always ask one of us "What is the business purpose of this meeting?" That was a very fair question, for which we did not always have an answer.

This book is intended to assist you in answering the question "Is this meeting really necessary?" with a powerful *yes* and to enable you as a project meeting facilitator to have your attendees leave your meetings with purpose, energy, and project actions in mind.

Both of us are longtime project management teachers and have discovered that repetition is good for the adult learner soul. So, if we say something and repeat it later in the book, that is intentional. Probably. Either that or it's a senior moment.

To aid you in your mission, the authors have created a select number of templates (e.g., risk register, RACI matrix), which you will be able to find on our website at http://projectmeetings.us.

We have also solicited war stories (trenchant stories from the trenches) from some of our colleague—and some from ourselves—and have sprinkled them throughout the book where they seemed appropriate. You will find them, we trust, both enlightening and amusing.

As to the title of the book, *Great Meetings Build Great Teams: A Guide for Project Leaders and Agilists,* we are not naïve enough to think that it is *only* great meetings that build teams. But they *are* a key factor.

We want to make it clear that this book is for both the traditional project managers and adherents of Agile. (The authors are both.) Servant leadership, which we consider part of the Agile mindset, is a "non-traditional leadership philosophy, embedded in a set of behaviors and practices that place a primary emphasis on the well-being of those being served." Those traits—servant leader traits—are exactly the traits one needs to be a good project meeting facilitator. (Not to mention a good project manager or agilist.)

The authors like to believe that they are your servant leaders through the wonderful world of meetings. And we believe this book will help you run better meetings whether you are working in a for-profit corporation, for a nonprofit, or even if you're on the dark side of the moon. (Apologies to Pink Floyd.)

Roadmap

The roadmap for this book is ... well, there *is* no roadmap to read this book *per se.* It is not a novel, so you don't have to start at the very beginning and read through to the end. You certainly can if you want and one of us (not Rich) is the kind of guy that feels he always has to.

We suggest this—peruse the table of contents and see if there is a particular situation you are dealing with right now. You could even jump immediately to our Appendix, which we call *Meeting Rules of the Road*. Virtual meetings? Chapter 9. Working in a multicultural environment? Chapter 8. Big Multiday project? Chapter 11? How to fly fish? Sorry, wrong book.

Lastly, you will occasionally see reference to a Glossary. So that we could provide you with the most content in this book, we have added a Glossry of terms used in this book in Appendix B. A downloadable version is also on our website at http://projectmeetings.us.*

Reference

Greenleaf, R. The Greenleaf Center for Servant Leadership. www.greenleaf.org/.

---

* Our glossary is very specific to terms in this book. If you are seeking more comprehensive glossaries, for waterfall we can suggest the Wideman Comparative Glossary of Project Management Terms www.maxwideman.com/pmglossary/ and for Agile, the Agile Alliance www.agilealliance.org/agile101/agile-glossary/.

CHAPTER 1

The Status of Projects Today

Key Takeaways

- Project management knowledge has grown; however, projects are not getting much more successful than decades ago.
- Planning improves a project's chance of success.
- Good communication and collaboration also contribute to project success.
- Project planning meetings (a form of communication and collaboration!) are at the heart of project success.

Book after project management book, report after project management report, study after project management study show that projects are not much more successful today than they were decades ago—depending, of course, on one's measure of success. One thing that's also been a common thread in books, reports, and studies is that better planning is one of the key differentiating factors in success versus failure. In today's world of tailored projects, planning may be geared toward using the predictive (waterfall), iterative (Agile), or both (hybrid) approach, but in any variation, planning is fundamental to the success of projects. Successful projects are not the result of Brownian motion (look it up!).

Allan Zucker (2016) has summarized the fairly depressing results of 20+ years of project success from The Standish Group's *CHAOS Report* surveys. The data show that there has been *no significant change in project success rates since 1994* (see Figure 1.1). Digging deeper, Zucker found some of the elements that *had* driven higher success rates, offering a few

CHART 1: LONGITUDINAL CHAOS RESEARCH

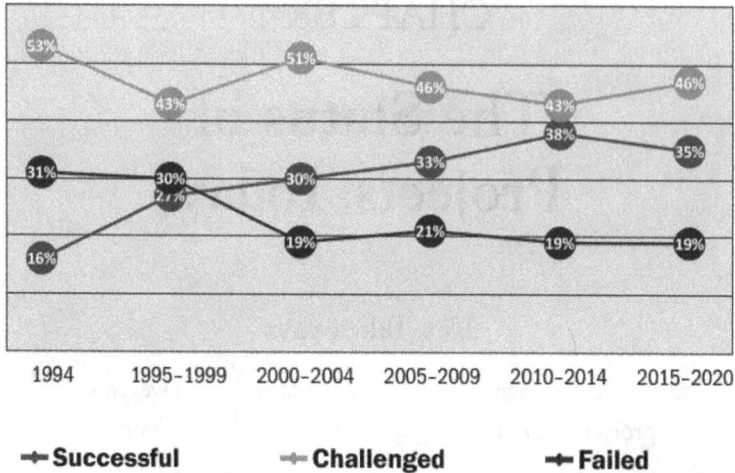

| | 1994 | 1995-1999 | 2000-2004 | 2005-2009 | 2010-2014 | 2015-2020 |

➤ **Successful**   ➤ **Challenged**   ➤ **Failed**

Figure 1.1 Standish Group's CHAOS reports show little change in project success over the years

rays of hope in these decades' worth of flat and drab results. Among those rays, he says that "teams that can *effectively communicate and collaborate* are better at resolving issues and solving problems."

Given the title of our book and our focus on how team dynamics contribute to successful meetings and successful projects, this is music to our ears. As is, say, Beethoven's Ninth Symphony, but that is again, a topic for a completely different book.

Standish is not the only group discussing these project problems or their effects on organizations. Take note of these statistics:

> "Eleven percent of investment is wasted due to poor project performance. And organizations that undervalue project management as a strategic competency for driving change report an average of 67 percent more of their projects failing outright."
>
> —*PMI Pulse of the Profession 2020 report*

How are projects being planned? Companies love Agile project management, but they adopt it piecemeal. According to the *15th Annual State of Agile Report*, the most popular Agile technique among businesses today is the daily standup, used by 87 percent of respondents. Runners-up include retrospectives (83 percent), sprint planning (83 percent), sprint review (81 percent), and short iteration cycles (63 percent).

Why so much emphasis on planning? Well, as you will see in the following chapters, there is evidence that planning is important to project success, and it's clear that meetings are—like them or not—needed for planning to take place. After all, few projects have only one team member, and even if they do, you may need a meeting with yourself from time to time. If you schedule such a meeting, please be sure to show up promptly, for goodness' sake.

The Project Management Institute's (PMI) *A Guide to the Project Management Body of Knowledge (PMBOK® Guide)—Sixth Edition* details 49 processes that should be performed to run a successful project. Almost half—24—are planning processes.

The Seventh Edition of the PMBOK® Guide* does away with the process groups, but it does *not* do away with planning. In fact, planning is one of the eight project performance domains, and is again highlighted in Section 4.6.3 of the Models, Methods, and Artifacts chapter. As to the Standard for Project Management (ANSI/PMI 99-001-2021), planning is featured in all 12 of its project management principles. PMI is conveying to us what carpenters have told us for decades: *measure twice, cut once.*

Lest you think that planning is unimportant in Agile, think again. Many Agile projects start out with a discovery or envisioning stage where ideas for the product or service are explored. Each sprint (a strict timebox itself) starts with a timebox for sprint planning where the team decides *what* it will accomplish in the sprint and *how* it will be accomplished. And while the main purpose of the sprint review is a demonstration, teams (and stakeholders) typically use it at least in part to plan the next sprint.

In terms of value for effort invested, planning is relatively easy to do and has lasting and worthwhile results, not only for the project, but—and this is key—for the project's *outcome*. The Wellingtone State of Project Management Report 2020 includes this figure (Figure 1.2), which shows

---

* PMI says that the Seventh Edition of the PMBOK® Guide does *not* replace the Sixth Edition, and that the Sixth Edition carries on in the form of PMI Standards+. This transition between Sixth and Seventh Edition is taking place as we write the book, so we encourage you to stay updated by going directly to PMI.org for the latest on the PMBOK® Guide and other Standards.

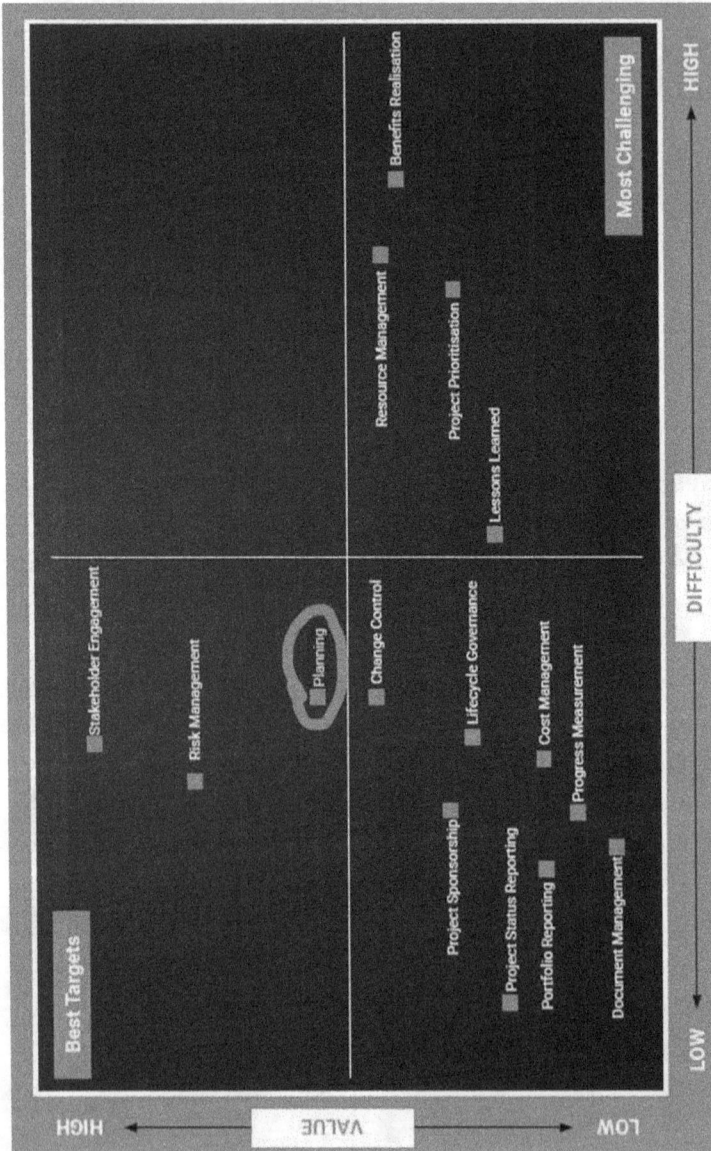

Figure 1.2 Where are the best targets for improving project success?

that the Best Targets for improving project success are planning, as well as risk and stakeholder management. All three of these be should a major focus for project leaders and, of course, for project meetings.

Despite the position of planning on this chart as one of the best targets, planning is not as well implemented as one might hope. The same Wellingtone report also shows that fewer than two-thirds of projects even *apply* a defined project methodology (Figure 1.3). So, there is room for improvement.

This book emphasizes planning—the very down-to-earth, nitty-gritty part of planning: project planning meetings. However, its principles can be used for the more mundane meetings such as status and lessons learned sessions, as well as the standup and retrospective meetings from the Agile approach. (Effectively, the Agile retrospective *is* a lessons learned session, just done more frequently.)

Whether the meeting is taking place in room 201A, just down the hall and on the left, on video screens worldwide, or in some combination of the nearby and the virtual, the project planning meeting is a staple of a project manager's world. Do you agree that—for a myriad of reasons, not the least of which is establishing a sense of *team*—planning is

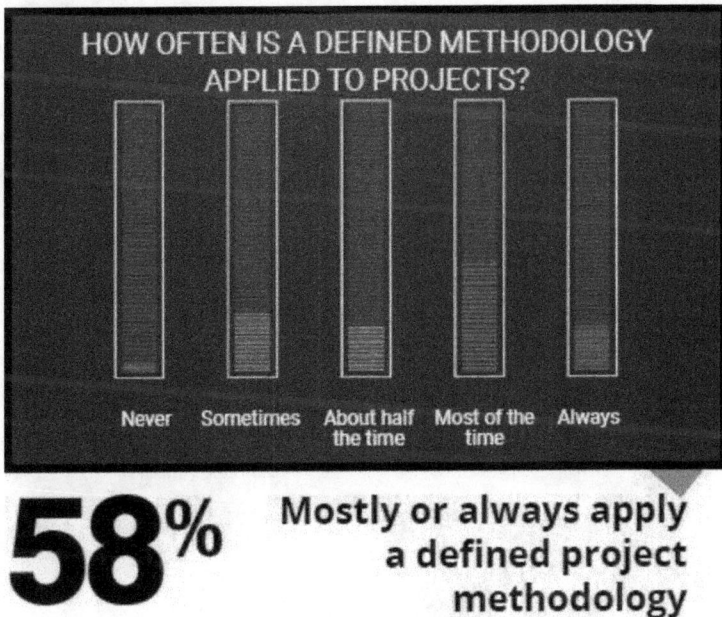

Figure 1.3 *Planning methodologies are not well deployed*

fundamental to project success? If so, you can understand that improved planning of meetings means better project results—and better delivery of value for the long term.

In this book, we'll cover kickoff meetings as well as project planning and status meetings in general and provide experience-based tips to help you facilitate effective, productive, interesting, and even—dare we say—*fun* project meetings—whatever the type.

Summary

You have seen evidence of the stagnant state of project success and the positive effect of planning, good communications, and collaboration on improvements to that success. As meetings are really at the intersection of communications and collaboration, we assert that improving your project meetings will improve the chance of success (and the reduction of stress) in your projects.

References

15th State of Agile Report—https://digital.ai/resource-center/analyst-reports/state-of-agile-report.

Standish: Johnson/Mulder *ENDLESS MODERNIZATION: How Infinite Flow Keeps Software Fresh*—provided by The Standish Group with permission to use figures.

Wellingtone: https://wellingtone.co.uk/wp-content/uploads/2020/06/The-State-of-Project-Management-Report-2020-Wellingtone.pdf.

CHAPTER 2

Take a Sad Meeting and Make It Better (With Apologies to the Beatles)

Key Takeaways

- Meetings have a bad reputation—deservedly so—for a variety of reasons, which we enumerate in the chapter. They also, surprisingly, have redeeming qualities.
- There are consequences of poor meetings, for the meeting itself, but also lasting consequences, in terms of diminished chances of project success.
- There is science behind the design of good meetings, and we highlight some of the key findings from research in this area.
- One key to good meeting design is acknowledging the role of team energy during the meeting. We provide tips on how to keep this energy present and positive.

No one really knows how the parties get to "Yes"
The pieces that are sacrificed in every game of chess
We just assume that it happens
But no one else is in the room where it happens
          —"The Room Where it Happens," from *Hamilton*,
          a musical by Lin-Manuel Miranda

The Status of Meetings Today

Meetings have a bad reputation. Often, they're a sad song. In many cases—okay, in most cases—they deserve this reputation, but not in all cases. We're here to try to show you what's wrong with them, how to make them better, and to improve their reputation—which in and of itself may just also make meetings better.

We can give you our opinion about what makes for bad meetings—and thus, their terrible reputation. We're reasonably sure you share some of these most hated things about meetings with us:

- The wrong people are there. You are missing key contributors, experts, knowledgeable people. You have extra people who don't need to be there or don't want to be there—or both.
- The meeting purpose is not clear. You hear it. Those murmurings in the back of the room. "Why are we here again?" "What are we doing here, anyway?" "This meeting always covers the same boring stuff, and nothing ever gets done."
- The meeting is all talk and no action. Even if the meeting arouses interest and excitement and people are proposing great new ideas and solutions, it's *not* always true that the idea will be germinated or if the solution will be implemented—or the decisions will be made.

A quick summary of what can be done about this (and you will see this theme—intentionally—repeated throughout this book) is:

- Project-manage your meetings. Be clear on your scope, your schedule, the budget of time, and the deliverables your meeting will produce.
- Focus on the agenda. The well-written agenda is the path to success for your meeting. It should be focused on engaging the right people on the most important topics. Use questions (more details on this coming) and plan productive discussions *into* the meeting.
- There's no meeting if there are no attendees. Well, of *course* there is no meeting without any attendees, but we make this ridiculous statement to make the larger point that there is no real chance for a successful meeting if the right attendees are not there for the topics in which they need to contribute and actively participate.

- Log the action items, assign, and confirm them. Record the decisions. Here's where, once again, you can rely on your project management skills. Like Dorothy in *The Wizard of Oz*, you had the power all along.

"Hold a meeting and make attendance optional. Then, you'll know who REALLY wants to be there."

—Daniel Mezick, Agile Coach

(We don't necessarily endorse this, but it is an interesting philosophy.)

There's much more about how to improve meetings later in this chapter. For now, let's continue to investigate their current state.

That Bad Reputation

Lucid Meetings is a creator of meeting management software. There is an excellent report from Lucidmeetings.com that covers highlights of meeting statistics (See Figure 2.1).

On average, how many meetings do you attend per week?

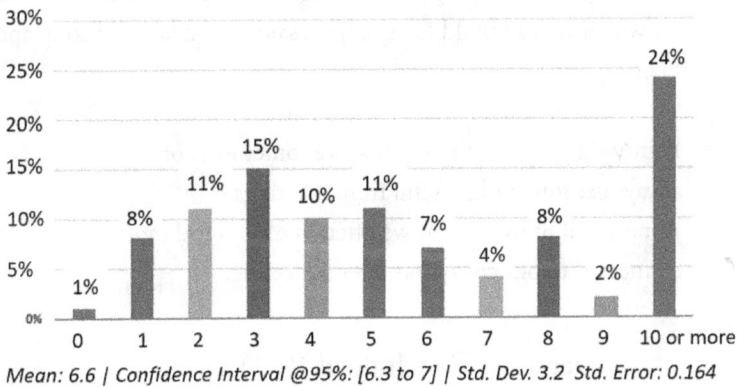

Mean: 6.6 | Confidence Interval @95%: [6.3 to 7] | Std. Dev. 3.2 Std. Error: 0.164

LUCID   lucidmeetings.com/state-of-meetings-2020

Figure 2.1 We attend many more meetings than we lead

Highlights from this report indicate that we're conflicted about meetings. It confirms our thinking that they have a bad reputation, although there are a few bright spots. Here are some examples from the dozens of excellent polls about meeting attendance, leadership, timing, and effectiveness, with a graphic example for the first poll and then, to save space, numeric data from the others. We look at some interesting findings next, with the supporting data, thanks to Lucidmeetings.com.

We attend many more meetings than we lead.

Contrast that with the answer to the poll question, "On average, how many meetings do you lead each week?" which had a mean of about 3.6 meetings.

We complain that meetings prevent us from doing "real work."

When asked to say how much this is true (and the possible answers Never, Rarely, Sometimes, Often, and Always), the result was a nicely symmetrical bell curve centered around Sometimes, with a 42 percent peak at Sometimes.

We get useful results from our meetings.

The same scale (Never, Rarely, Sometimes, Often, and Always) was used for this statement. The results indicate another bell curve, this time centered between Sometimes and Often.

Our meetings help me feel connected with my coworkers.

Again, using the same scale as earlier, the results were a sharp bell curve centered between Sometimes and Often.

So, we can see that among all of the bad news, here are some of the things on which we can build (after all, we said we'd take a sad song and make it better):

- Eighty-six percent of us say that we sometimes, often, or always get something useful from meetings.
- Almost half of us say that we often or always feel more connected to our coworkers after a meeting.

Meetings Can Indeed Be Wasteful

Following is an infographic from Fuze.com (Figure 2.2) that provides some of the statistics that indicate the current state of meetings.

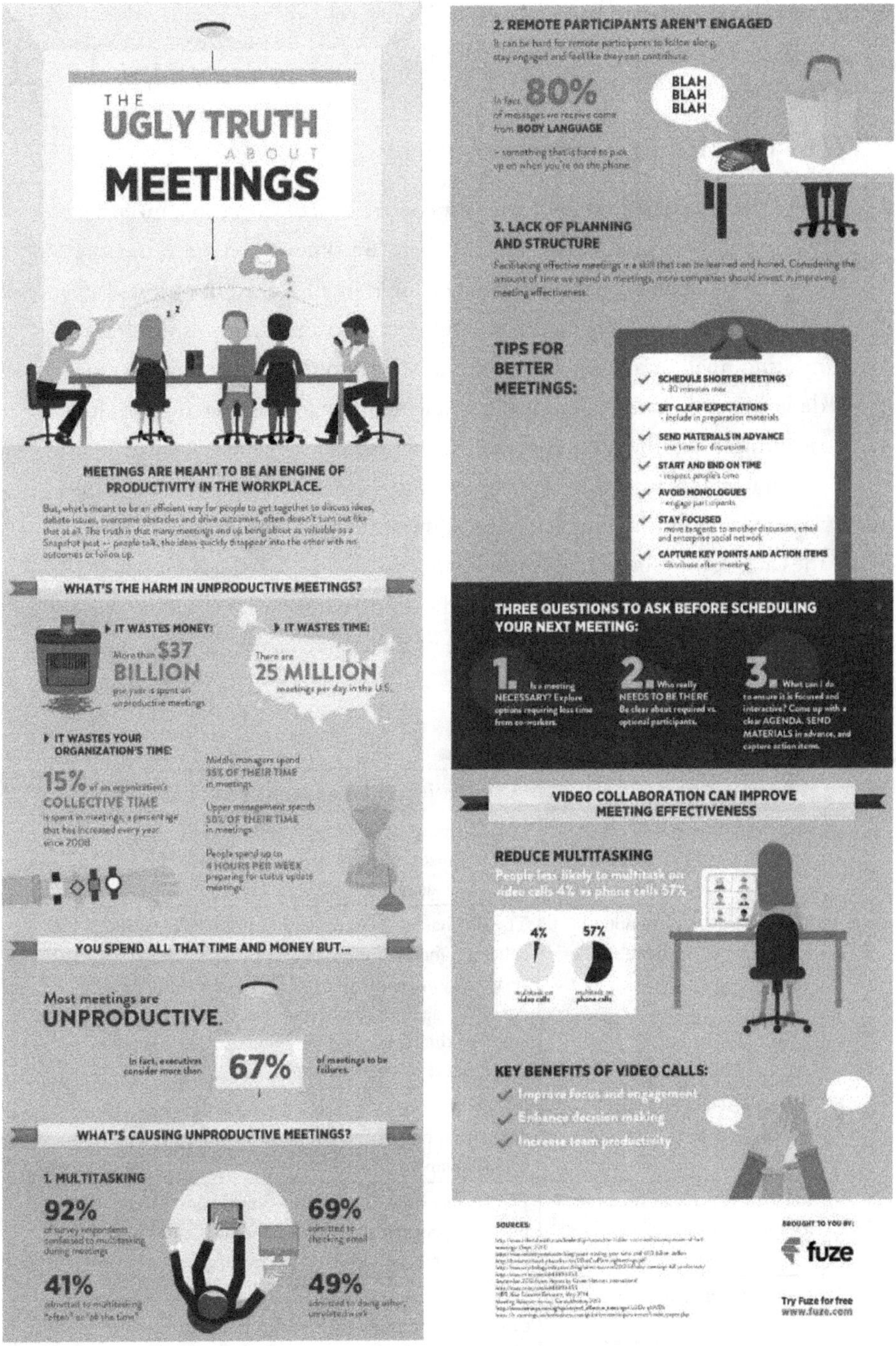

Figure 2.2 The Ugly Truth About Meetings (courtesy of Fuze.com)

Okay, now that we've established the problem, we can start with analysis and response. We begin with this question.

Are Bad Meetings a Symptom or a Cause?

When was the last time that you just could *not wait* to get to a meeting? We know from personal experience there are times when we count the minutes (or even hours) until the meeting is finally called to a close. But do you recall counting the days, hours, minutes, and seconds until that meeting finally started? Probably not. The reason? The meetings weren't designed well. And this can spell trouble not only for the meeting, but for the project (and by extension, the organization).

In fact, it may be the other way around. Perhaps the poor meetings are a symptom of something larger, in addition to (or even instead of) being the cause. Also, some people just simply do *not* like meetings. Hopefully, you can be part of the solution—and turn that around for them.

Next, we have summarized some of the characteristics of poor meetings and separately, the possible causes of these characteristics (Figures 2.3 and 2.4).

The meeting itself	Project management root cause
Meeting purpose is unclear	Project's purpose is unclear or unpopular and/ or the project manager has not done a good job of setting an agenda.
The right people are not expressing their thoughts	The PM has not set proper ground rules for team behavior and/or some people are uncomfortable speaking up, and/or the project manager (see next) doesn't have the right people at the right meetings, and that they are engaged, giving the meeting the proper level of attention and focus.
Wrong people are invited/ missing people	Project has not identified proper stakeholder population or PM has not made a compelling case for attendance.
Inadequate time allowed for meeting	Project priorities (the order of constraints) has not been properly determined and/or the PM has allowed someone to hijack the meeting.
Poorly designed agenda (or no agenda)	Project's communication management plan is absent or lacking and/or project manager is ineffective at planning meetings
Meeting facility is unsuitable (noise/capacity)	

Figure 2.3 Poor meetings and project root causes

Consequence for the meeting itself	Consequence for the project
Project being disconnected from mission/vision of organization	Project management success (on schedule, under budget, scope met) but project failure (the project doesn't deliver what was really needed by key stakeholders).
Incompletely capturing scope/risk	Project doesn't deliver what was promised or delivers what the PM *thought* was promised (which ... isn't what was promised).
Undervalued team members or a feeling that their opinion doesn't count	Lost key input (potentially critical subject matter expert (SME) input) and alienated team members and failing to be alerted about a disastrous threat to the project or its product.
Team member feels that the meeting didn't go well*	Establish precedent for poor communications and team dynamics for the remainder of the project (not just meetings).
Confusion	Alienation, people leaving the project, and significant potential for waste and rework.
Unidentified risks	No risk response plan, resulting use of much duct tape and WD-40 (or the equivalent adhesives and lubricants).
Gaps in budget, resource, schedule	No means to—or at least a delay in—requesting increases in needed resources, budget, or time.
Conflict and arguing at the meeting	The downside: if it is personalized this will likely yield alienation and people leaving the team or providing *sarcastic compliance*.
	The upside: if the conflict is *tamed* and handled so that it is focused on issues, conflict can be a driver of creativity and passion.
Meeting is argumentative and combative	Team members depart or *shut down*. The bad reputation of meetings (at least your meetings) is promulgated.

Figure 2.4 Consequences of poor meetings

War Story From a Colleague—An Insufficiently Compelling Case to Attend

I once scheduled a meeting with an international vendor, to demonstrate a QA/QC software tool to the management team (approximately fourteen people, representing seven departments that would

---

* The authors have observed that every organization seems to have a grumpy person who takes it on as their point of pride to go to meetings, arms folded, and with a severe frown, repeatedly says, "This will never work", followed by, "We tried this before, it was a dismal failure". We're not sure what drives this behavior, but it is out there.

be required to use the tool). The vendor was on time, I was on time, the room was setup, but no one else appeared. After 15 minutes of making awkward small talk, I apologized profusely, promised to reschedule, and went searching for the team.

Turns out, sometime after I scheduled the demo meeting, someone announced a birthday party in the breakroom. So, fourteen managers and directors did not show up for a software demo (in an industry where QC is required by law) instead choosing to go to a birthday party. One of them was bold enough to confront me and state "Next time you schedule a meeting, be sure the alternative doesn't include cake."

—Michael Pace, PhD, via LinkedIn

We have shown you what other people think—what has been found through polls and research. Now, let's internalize that. Ask yourself: besides great snacks, what entices you to attend a meeting (as a team member, not as a project manager)? Really. Take a deep breath, right now. Why do *you* want to attend a particular meeting?

- You want to contribute.
- You want to be sure a key point is made.
- You want to express a creative idea.
- You enjoy the social aspect.
- You want to be updated on the project's progress.
- You are intensely invested in the outcome of the project.

Now turn this around and think about this from the meeting planner perspective. Understanding the team's motivation for attending, and what will make them get the most out of the meeting will assist you in getting more productive (and enjoyable) use of the team participants, leading to a more productive, fun, and interesting meeting.

"Because there's consequences for what we do… Consequences for me and you."

—bluesman Robert Cray

Effects (Consequences) of Poor Meetings

Note that these consequences from meeting ineffectiveness yield the exact opposite of typical critical success factors (CSFs) for projects. They become critical failure factors (CFFs), an acronym we just made up[†], and which we feel could be very successful in measuring failures!

Later in this chapter, we reveal some of the findings of Dr. Steven Rogelberg. He talks about something quite related to CFFs called Meeting Recovery Syndrome (MRS)[‡], which comprises the time and energy spent after frustrating meetings often including destructive commiseration with colleagues (Rogelberg 2019). As to CSFs, our Glossary has an example showing the linkage between objectives, CSFs and key performance indicators (KPIs). For now, know that a CSF describes the way in which you will get to that success criteria—so think of a CSF as the means to the end.

So, those meeting statistics are significantly depressing. They describe a current state that is unacceptable. We need to get to a future state in which meetings are seen in a better light, are productive, have a good reputation, and even (gasp!) are looked forward to.

War Story—A Project That Forgot Its Main Deliverable

Let me set the scene for you. It is literally *right* before the COVID-19 pandemic. I was asked to sit in on a dedicated design review session that was not a project I was actually on, so I wasn't sure what it was about. The project manager has the design drawings displayed on a large screen in the front of the room. We get to the in-scope plan drawing, which is the actual plan view of the room where work is happening. The project manager is discussing the plans for a new fume hood they are putting in and how the new fume hood required a new fume exhaust system, so that is being put in.

---

† Actually, we discovered that although we thought we made this up, the term has been used before. See: https://papers.ssrn.com/sol3/papers.cfm?abstract_id=3072157.

‡ www.mentimeter.com/blog/stay-current-with-mentimeter/study-finds-meetings-in-the-united-states-to-be-routinely-underprepared.

What she does not discuss is the *Nederman arm* (a flexible vapor-extraction hose) that is in the center of the room. Before we move on to the next drawing she asks, "Any questions?" And one gentleman (who is a blue-collar guy based on his blue maintenance uniform and clearly the low man in the room) says "What about my arm? That's what I approached you about and you said you would replace it with this project."

The project manager paused and literally just looked defeated. She said, "I forgot about your arm." And so, she turns to the mechanical engineer and asks if there is enough budget left to replace the arm. And I'm thinking to myself, there *better* be! This man asked for an arm, and you decided a fume hood and new exhaust system were more important? Ultimately, it was decided there was budget, luckily, based on some taxes they didn't have to pay.

The big kicker ... we turn to the next drawing, and there is the arm in the room with a huge out of scope on it, while the entire rest of the room was in scope. Everyone laughed (a nervous laugh though).

At the end of the meeting, I end up blurting out "How did this happen? How did a project that was intended to replace the arm turn into not actually replacing the arm?" And the project manager says, "Well not everyone comes to all the meetings." What?! He's an hourly worker, he *can't* come to all these meetings. How did she lose sight of the original scope of the project so badly?! I have no clue. I'm guessing a big part of it is that she's not actually a project manager but a scientist who was *dubbed* project manager. (Deep collective sigh here from your authors.)

—Anonymous, from a project manager at a pharmaceutical product manufacturing department

Let's Talk About How to Turn This Around and Make Project Meetings Better!

The Importance of Good Meeting Design

Meetings can create great outcomes if you want them to: new ideas, better strategies, stronger relationships, good decisions, and

organizational changes. These outcomes come from being intentional with the time you spend together. Meeting design is the practice of expressing that intention.

—from *Meeting Design* by Kevin Hoffman
www.amazon.com/dp/B0754NL9R3/ref=dp-
kindle-redirect?_encoding=UTF8&btkr=1.

There's Some Science Here

Few people have focused on the science of meetings. We found some who have—and we want to share their findings with you.

Dr. Steven Rogelberg and Dr. John Jokello have investigated this for decades. Dr. Rogelberg published a book in 2019 called *The Surprising Science of Meetings*. It's highly recommended reading. See our references at the end of the chapter for two videos in which Professors Rogelberg and Jokello discuss their book, and one in which Professor Rogelberg reviews the highlights of his book with employees at Google.

We've gleaned some of the top points from Rogelberg's book here, and put our own project leadership twist on them:

- There are about one hundred million daily meetings globally, and all are about the same as each other. So, do whatever you can as a project leader to make your meetings different.
- Avoid proliferating the myth that meetings are just—by nature—terrible, because:
  ○ It's not true.
  ○ It's an easy excuse to not even try to improve them.
  ○ It's a trap you can avoid by following the advice in this book.
- Frame agenda items as questions.
- Be creative in the meeting design. Example: allow moments of silence—pauses—to allow those perhaps more introverted participants to speak.
- Pick the start time for your meeting with intent—that is, tactically—and keep the meeting short, tight by design.
- Avoid defaulting to any standard timeframe (typically 30 or 60 minutes). Parkinson's law dictates that work adjusts to fill the time allotted.

- Think about the variety of attendees you have and plan accordingly.
- To make your meetings better, ask those who regularly attend what *they* think would make the meeting better.
- Positive energy, gratitude, and appreciation, producing a contagion effect, promote a chance for increased active listening.
- Think of your meeting as a movie script: it needs a hook, something that draws people to attend and makes it memorable.
- Whatever is discussed in the first five minutes is going to get the most attention. After that, people will pretty much be sound asleep, or loafing‡—especially if you ignore the coaching in our book.

> Another finding from Rogelberg's research: *Highly conscientious individuals* are the *most pleased when a meeting goes well,* and *most upset when the meeting does not serve the purpose.* Interestingly, project managers tend to be highly conscientious.

This was first identified when French agricultural engineer and later, Professor Max Ringelmann noticed that individuals pulling on a rope worked harder than when they were assigned this task in a team.

Another lens through which we can look at project meetings is the effect of pressure on the success of teams—and in particular, teams in meetings.

---

‡ *Loafing* is an American colloquialism, which has nothing to do with bread and everything to do with hanging around at leisure, pretty much doing nothing. *Social loafing* refers to the concept that people are prone to exert less effort when working collectively as part of a group compared to performing a task alone. Social loafing is more evident in tasks where the contribution of each group member is combined into group outcome, making it difficult to identify the contribution of a single person.

Be Sensory—Not Sen-Sorry

As meetings are so important, and as communication and collaboration (the heart of any meeting) are a way out of the lackluster success rate of projects, you can sense the importance of holding planning meetings. In fact, let's dwell on the *senses* for a moment. All of them. We like to say, "Be sensory—not sen-sorry." We encourage you to use your senses of sight, sound, taste, touch, and smell to help drive successful planning meetings for your project.

We're not talking literally about sight, sound, taste, touch, and smell—we've taken some liberty with the words describing the senses here—using more expanded definitions of the words—more colloquial definitions. Now, don't be too sensitive about that!

- **See the Light**
  Your project has been chartered—or so we assume—at this point. So, you know what the end result should look like. Now you not only need to keep the end in mind, but you also need to keep your team's eyes on that end—the proverbial "light at the end of the tunnel." This means that during planning, you should be constantly refining the project's objectives.

  If your project has a visual outcome (such as a new hospital wing a bridge, even a book or software application), keep an image of the finished project product in sight of the team as much as possible. This is the goal, "the light at the end of the tunnel." So don't let your team work—or meet— in the dark. Light the way with whatever it is that your project will provide the organization.

- **Keep in Touch**
  We use the expression "keep in touch" to remind you—as a planner—that the planning process can only be successful if all who contribute or care about the project know its appropriate details—ground rules, expectations, methods, tools. In fact, we have always asserted that in any e-mail communication—and particularly in terms of meeting

announcements and notes from meetings—the distribution
list is as important as the content.

Even the notification method you use for the meeting may
need to vary depending on the audience. For example, some
people will want (or need) a voice message or text in addition
to an e-mail invitation. The right people (and only the right
people) should know about the meetings, the purpose of the
meetings, the expectations of the meeting outcome, and,
especially, any actions for them that come from the meeting.
Overcommunication is not necessarily a bad thing.

No Accounting for Taste

Here we use the word *taste* in the sense of "there's no accounting for
taste"—in other words, a reference to choices of style, fashion, even of
significant others—*that* sort of taste. This can serve as a reminder that:

- There's often more than one style of planning.
- Your team will have their own tastes when it comes to how
  they are involved in planning, meeting styles and format, and
  communications styles. Seek input from them in advance of
  the meeting for such preferences. Listen to these views, and
  consider them all in your decisions, but remember, you are in
  charge as the project manager, and you make these decisions.
- Your team may have a variety of preferences when it comes to
  distributing planning information (see *Touch*)
- People are not inside your head. Don't assume they all think
  like you or share the same enthusiasm you do for your project.
  As likely as not, they have several other concurrent projects,
  and this is, for them, just another one—and your meeting (if
  you are not careful—is just another boring meeting).

The Sweet Smell of Success

Here we talk of sense of smell akin to the abilities of a hound dog—the
means to sniff out threats and opportunities. We need a complete capture of
two things in particular at the early planning stages: stakeholders and risks.

It is imperative that these be fully sniffed out so that this list is complete.§ A failure to identify a stakeholder means that all of the value this stakeholder could provide is absent—or that the dangers that may come with this stakeholder won't be considered.

- **Hear Ye, Hear Ye…**
  The expression "having your ear to the ground," originating from the technique of placing one ear to the ground to detect movement of animals or people from a distance, is all about being well aware of trends, opinions, and even rumors. The way any project manager can do this is to use management by walking around (MBWA) or Gemba Walk.**

  Be aware of the latest *news* about your project and the project team (even on a personal level). Who just had a child or grandchild? Did someone have a skiing accident and now will be out for a few weeks? Are they attending a rock *n* roll camp where they will schmooze with (and play) rock star for a couple of days? (Like one of us—not Rich—did).

Synthesizing the Sensory Information

Now that you have gathered all of this sensory information, it's up to your command center (your brain!) to synthesize and organize it into knowledge. You will use your information and your project management know how, to determine, for example:

- How you will identify, analyze, and respond to risk.
- How you will identify, engage with, and manage stakeholders.

---

§ We are talking about a complete, broad, and deep identification of stakeholders, threats, and opportunities for the project but also for your meetings!
** In lean manufacturing, the idea of *Gemba* is that the problems are visible, and the best improvement ideas will come from going to the Gemba—a Japanese word for "the real place." The *Gemba* Walk, much like management by walking around (MBWA), is an activity that takes management to the front lines to look for waste and opportunities to practice *Gemba* kaizen, or practical shop floor improvement. An important difference with MBWA is that Gemba Walks are not done randomly, but with a clear goal and often frequency and structure.

- How you'll acquire resources.
- How you'll communicate.
- How you'll lead and develop the team.
- How you'll set and manage scope.
- How you'll determine, baseline the schedule and budget.
- There are others—be sure you customize this list for your projects.

Fixing that bad reputation: What *is* a successful project meeting? It has a lot to do with energy.

If we are to repair the bad reputation of project meetings, we then need to understand what a successful project meeting really is.

According to Valkenburg et al. (*Five Frustrations of Project Managers*), "an effective project meeting sees participants leave with fresh insights and energy, generated through confidence in the direction of the project and each other." In fact, they have an entire chapter dedicated to project meetings—indeed, project meetings constitute one of the five frustrations of the project manager.

This is where planning and meetings intersect—in the form of planning *for* meetings (Figure 2.5). "A lack of focus on preparation can lead to the meeting itself costing a lot of time and being characterized by negative

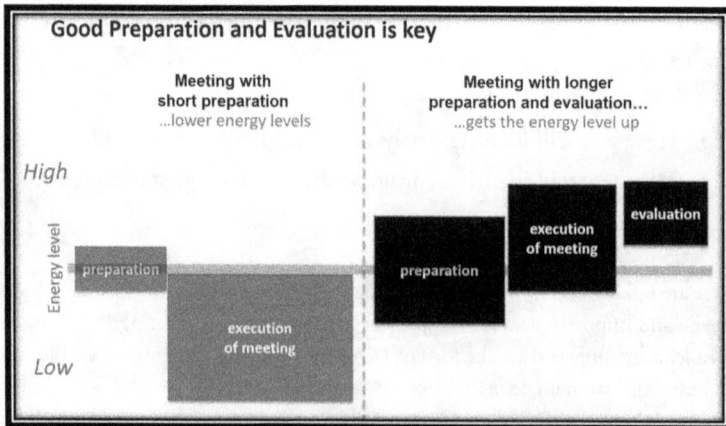

Figure 2.5 Good preparation and evaluation is key

energy. In our experience a greater focus on preparation than on execution improves the quality and results of (project) meetings."

We started this chapter with some statistics from Lucid Meetings illustrating that the *Current State* of meetings displays such a missed opportunity, with the commensurate bad reputation. We've given you some advice as to how to get to the *Future State* in which meetings are indeed looked on with positivity, and people actually do look forward to participating in them—and they do provide the value they should.

We end with one more tip from Lucid Meetings, and that is the concept of establishing a working team agreement. They have two flavors: *in person* and *remote*. Read more about them below—and note the templates that are available as well:

In person: www.lucidmeetings.com/templates/how-create-working-team-agreement.

Remote: www.lucidmeetings.com/templates/how-create-remote-team-working-agreement.

Summary

In this chapter, we have reminded you (as if you needed it) that meetings can be a really sad song, and as such, they develop a bad reputation, which can make them worse. It's a cacophonous death spiral. (Cacophonous Death Spiral would be a great name for a band.) We provided some science and research-based tips that can hopefully reverse that situation and move us to a *future state* in which meetings get more productive, more effective, more participative, and in turn, their reputation advances—as does your projects' chances of success.

References

About Social Loafing and the Ringelmann Effect: www.simplypsychology.org/social-loafing.html.

How to create a working team agreement: www.lucidmeetings.com/templates/how-create-working-team-agreement.

Lucid Meetings info: www.lucidmeetings.com/state-of-meetings-2020

Rogelberg, S.G. 2019. *The Surprising Science of Meetings: How You Can Lead Your Team to Peak Performance*. Oxford University Press.
Videos from Rogelberg and Jokello—The Science of Meetings:

- https://youtu.be/W0Vs-SchrAg
- https://youtu.be/FWIlZosXxCM

www.forbes.com/sites/peterhigh/2019/11/25/half-of-all-meetings-are-a-waste-of-timeheres-how-to-improve-them/?sh=7d9640202ea9\
www.metisstrategy.com/interview/steven-rogelberg/.

CHAPTER 3

The Importance of Planning, Meetings, and Planning Your Meetings

Plans are worthless, but planning is everything.
—Dwight D. Eisenhower

Key Takeaways

- A plan is static. Planning is more about *design* and *intent*. Planning is dynamic, alive, and well informed. Think *planning*, not plans.
- You already apply planning to your projects—something you do almost instinctively because it results in better projects. Just shift this mindset over to your meetings!
- The effort spent in planning project meetings pays off in tangible and intangible ways.

As planning is everything, we want to dedicate a proper portion of coverage to this topic and be sure that you have the motivation and tools to do it right.

NOTE: As project managers, we sometimes get myopic about certain words, and plan is one of them. We sometimes think of a plan as a timeline or Gantt chart. In this chapter, when we refer to the noun *plan*, we are referring to a document that identifies the background and steps to get something done, not a timeline, milestone, or Gantt chart. That's a *schedule*, or as our British friend Peter Taylor would say, SHEDule.

Planning Is Dynamic

We begin by asserting the difference between *a plan* and *planning*. We are discussing the importance of planning. What may appear to be a trivial difference is actually quite significant, as best expressed by Jack Duggan (2012) in his paper, *Managing the DANCE: Think Design, Not Plan*.

The DANCE to which Duggan refers is an acronym for dynamic and changing, ambiguous and uncertain, nonlinear, and unpredictable, complex, and emergent—this is the nature of projects today. (Emergent is an important word, especially to the agilists.) So, having a plan (the noun) means that you have created something static. By shifting to the word planning—we take into account that the plan will need to evolve.

Project planning is indeed an ongoing process, whether the methodology is waterfall or Agile. (We'll define those terms later.) And as projects DANCE more now than ever before, that means planning is more important now than ever before.

Planning Makes a Difference

Andy Crowe's book, *Alpha Project Managers: What The Top 2% Know That Everyone Else Does Not* (2016), summarizes a landmark survey of over 800 project managers to find out what the top 2 percent (the alphas) do that other project managers do not. A key finding: alpha project managers spent twice as much time in the planning phase of their projects than did nonalphas.

Does planning make a difference? Yes, significantly. In his paper, *The Importance of the Planning Phase to Project Success*, author Pedro Serrador (2012) wrote about the correlation of project success with the effort put forth upfront (and ongoing) in planning projects. Among his conclusions:

- Pressure exists in the project environment to reduce the time spent planning rather than increase it.
- The level of planning completeness is positively correlated with project success in the construction industry.
- Planning is associated with project success, in terms of both project efficiency and overall project success.

So, although there will be pressure to do without planning, look at the compelling reasons to achieve what Serrador calls *planning completeness*. This will, in turn, require project planning meetings. That brings us to the importance of the meetings themselves and the compelling need to do them right or not at all.

Pick any major event, trip, or undertaking in your life and think about the time, energy, and work put into making sure everything went off without a hitch. Then think about the stress and aggravation you experienced those times when things didn't go as desired. Doesn't your project warrant at least as much planning as, say, your upcoming vacation to the Netherlands to catch the cheese festival in Alkmaar? Or your long-delayed trip to the *Burning Man* Festival?

As a discipline, project management for your professionally run projects works the same way as for vacation projects, except on a greater scale and involving more stakeholders and a larger pool of resources. It can include external vendors, several other internal and intradepartmental team members (as well as their schedules and input), additional parameters such as cost, quality, timing, constant coordination and communication, and associated risks.

Without planning, projects suffer from:

- Lack of strategic alignment
- Cost, quality, and time-constraint issues and scope creep
- Lack of stakeholder engagement and commitment
- Inefficient use of resources
- Frustration, morale, and conflict in the project team
- Communication issues
- Botched risk responses

Here is the important connection for this book: meetings are so prolific in the workplace that they fly under the radar and are not thought of as what they actually are: mini-events, mini-projects in and of themselves. Meetings deserve the same sort of thoughtful planning as do your projects!

Keep in mind that things may have changed significantly postpan-demic. Witness this paragraph from PMI's President Mike DiPrisco, writing in *Forbes* magazine in April 2022.

When bringing employees back to the office, be intentional. Leaders need to give employees strong reasons why in-person interactions work best in a particular situation. They must also recognize that physical offices are likely to serve a different purpose now than in the past. For many organizations, they will become meeting places for workshopping new ideas, recruiting and customer interactions, as well as rallying points where culture and identity are reinforced. Creating such spaces can be linked directly to better business outcomes. According to (PMI's) research as published in Forbes magazine, high-performing, "front-runner" organizations are much likelier to say their project managers have strong relationship-building and collaborative leadership skills compared with average companies.

Meetings (at least face-to-face meetings) have gained importance postpandemic, and serve a varied, more important set of purposes aside from the already important role they played (if properly facilitated) before.

Given that meetings have gained importance, and given the importance of planning, we assert, and hope you agree, that thoughtful planning of meetings is effort well spent. Take the time to plan your meetings, and it will pay off in tangible ways (meetings that run more quickly, get action items accomplished, and decisions made) and intangible ways (stronger, more cohesive teams and higher morale in your project teams).

NOTE: In the interest of acknowledging alternative viewpoints, there is a concept called Open Space, which has arisen out of the Agile world. One of the authors attended a virtual Open Space meeting and found it to be interesting if hard to place exactly in context for his own project world.

According to the Agile Alliance, in open space meetings, participants create and manage their own agenda of parallel sessions around a specific theme. Participants are invited to build the event schedule, just-in-time. Individuals propose sessions they'd like to lead, or sessions they'd like to see someone else step up and lead. Quickly, almost if by magic, a schedule emerges, composed of sessions around topics people feel passionate about pursuing.

Like Agile itself, open space technology sessions operate under a small set of guiding principles. These principles are deceptively simple, yet provide just enough structure for spontaneous discussions:

- Whoever comes are the right people.
- Whatever happens is the only thing that could have.
- Whenever it starts is the right time.
- Whenever it's over, it's over.
- Wherever it happens is the right place.

Or as the Beatles famously said in "All You Need Is Love": *There's nowhere you can be that isn't where you're meant to be.*

You can find out more at Open Space World
https://openspaceworld.org/wp2/what-is/.

Summary

You have been presented with the challenge of applying the same planning mindset you use for improved project success to your meetings. We assert that this will result in tangible and intangible benefits, which we list in the chapter. Think of your meeting as an event—a project—and design and plan it that way. It will make a difference.

References

Forbes interview with then PMI president Mike DiPrisco
Source: www.forbes.com/sites/forbesbusinesscouncil/2022/04/15/moving-into-
the-great-rejuvenation-of-work-leadership-must-step-up.

CHAPTER 4

The Zen of Facilitation

Key Takeaways

🗨 We define and stress the importance of facilitation and your role as a facilitator when it comes to running a project meeting.

🗨 We provide facilitation tips under what we call The Zen of Facilitation.

🗨 We introduce you to the meeting goblins—personalities you may already have encountered but for whom you now have names—and ways in which you can deal with these meeting disruptors.

Merriam-Webster defines *facilitate* as "to make something easier" or "to help something run more smoothly or effectively." And while the second definition is more to the point, we like the first one too. When you run even a one-hour meeting, you are facilitating—the same thing you are trying to accomplish in a larger two-day summit meeting. You're trying to move the meeting along, make it run more smoothly, limit sidebar conversations, achieve the meeting objectives, and so on.

It's not altogether unlike the role of servant leader, in which you are there not to direct, to control, to command, but rather to be sure roadblocks are removed, that the conversation is cared for, and that the outcome of the meeting—including the satisfaction of the participants—is positive.

But this isn't an easy task, nor is it a skill we're born with. And your success with a meeting will be greatly determined not only by the planning you've done but also by the way that you run the session. A well-planned, poorly run meeting not only won't help, but it may well hurt and cause you to be discredited before you even start. Remember, as a project manager, you plan and execute projects, and as we've said earlier, a meeting is a project. So, you will be (consciously or subconsciously) judged not only as a meeting facilitator but as a project manager based on how well your meetings go. We focus on project meeting facilitation here. With a simple search, you can find many books which cover the general topic more generically.

Facilitation skills really come into play when you are planning a big gathering with a diverse group of stakeholders. For the sake of discussion, let's assume this is a project planning meeting of at least one day. This is one area where you will have to shine and where the herding of cats will not be trivial.

Distinguishing Being a Facilitator From Using a Facilitative Style

This is where the Zen comes in. As defined by the Zen Studies Society, Zen is: *"something we are—our true nature expressing itself moment by moment—and something we do—a disciplined practice through which we can realize the joy of being."*

So, practicing Zen in facilitation means that it's something we *are* (being a facilitator) and *do* (using a facilitation style).

Facilitators serve as guides, leaders, and enablers:

- They play an important part in a well-run meeting by ensuring that the meeting is productive, focused, inclusive, and effective.
- They have skills in planning agendas, creating productive group environments, developing appropriate group processes, encouraging participation, and leading the group to reach its desired outcomes.

Instructors or leaders using a facilitative style are guides, instigators, partners, and leaders are:

- Experts in both content and process.
- Tasked to ensure that the participants' direction and decisions are on target.
- Responsible for motivating participants and creating a positive environment for the exchange of ideas and knowledge.

Facilitation Tips

- Sounding almost Zen-like itself, we invoke the concept of begin with the end in mind. This is a concept Stephen Covey developed in his book *The Seven Habits of Highly Effective People.* If you keep your goals in mind during the meeting and remind the group of what they are on a regular basis, you'll increase your chances of success. Do not allow yourself to be sidetracked or the meeting hijacked.
- Be—or delegate to—a timekeeper. You have an agenda, and to the extent that it's humanly possible, you must get through it. Be firm about the time without being needlessly harsh. If something requires 15 extra minutes, make a judgment call as to whether or not to allow it. Then adjust the agenda accordingly.
- Set expectations. This should have been done premeeting. Do what salespeople and good instructors do—tell them what you're going to tell them, tell them, then tell them what you told them.
- In line with setting expectations, set ground rules. This could include how long people get the floor (see *Meeting Goblins,* next) and guidelines for breaks, laptop, and cell use, and starting right on time even if all are not present.
- Be large and in charge, without being bold and prone to scold. Facilitating a meeting with a large group, some of whom may be senior to you, isn't for the faint of heart. Act like you belong there because you do. This is your party. A show of confidence is important and, oddly, can build more confidence. People are looking for leadership.

- Don't worry about being liked. This isn't Facebook, and you're not seeking approbation. If you say to yourself, "If I stop this conversation, they won't like me," you're the wrong person not only for the facilitation role but perhaps also for a project manager job.
- Be sure to focus on behavior, not the person. This can be done assertively, but without confrontation. As Zen practitioners might say, vow to live with attention, integrity, and authenticity.
- Be a good listener. People need to be heard. Listen to them and don't just wait for your opening to speak. Try active listening, where you paraphrase back what they've said.
- Resolve conflict. This is one of the tougher ones. Sometimes, conflicts are of a long-standing nature, have nothing to do with the meeting, and aren't going to be *resolved* in this meeting. You and the sponsor should have discussed this in advance. Conflict doesn't necessarily (or even) mean that tempers flare. Conflict is to be expected, and as long as it's about issues and not personal, it can be very good for innovation and problem-solving.
- If tempers *do* flare, call for a break, even if you've just had one. This is a differently purposed break.
- Keep the conversation interesting. Some people will come to the meeting expecting to be bored to tears, especially in a day-long or multiday meeting. Prevent this from happening. Engage them. Get stimulating conversation going about the product or the project. Use (very short) stories as appropriate. Both authors teach and can advise you that students are always surprised by how interesting project management is. Inherently, it's not. You have to *make* it interesting. This arises only with good planning and execution of a meeting. And, frankly, if you're not a dull, monotonic speaker.
- Consider taking a presentation skills class. Both authors have done so, and found the feedback—from both class and instructor—invaluable, and now include that in our own coaching and mentoring.
- Be flexible. Remember how we said that you should have an agenda and that you must stick to it? Well, sure. But don't be afraid to tear it up or revise it mid-stream if you think

adjustments need to be made. As Zen practitioners may say, *"release us from the shackles of past and future, as well as from the self-imposed and imprisoning barriers we erect around what we erroneously consider our separate and unchanging identities."* (Don't worry—that's about as philosophical as we get.)

An Ex-Zen-Ple

One of the authors worked for a woman who was expert in facilitation. With the key stakeholders, we would plan an agenda for a two-day planning meeting. The goal of the meeting was to produce several artifacts—work breakdown structures, a draft schedule, lists of risks and issues, and an action list.

Midway through the first day of the session, things were not going as planned. It turned out that the requirements for the medical device were not quite as well developed as we had been led to believe. So, she turned to the author and said, "We are going to re-do the agenda." We advised the audience that we needed a break, went into another room with the sponsor, tore up the agenda, and wrote a new one on the fly. We didn't get every single artifact we wanted and saved those for follow-up sessions. But boy, did we understand the requirements. And the author learned a valuable lesson.

- Seek neutrality. As likely as not, you're an internal employee working in a specific department. So, strictly speaking, 100 percent neutrality is impossible. Unless you hire an outside facilitator, try to wear the other group's hat as well as your own. The sponsor can help here. Once again, from our Zen friends, the concept of kuu (空): *Find the perfect middle ground without leaning in any specific directions. When you reach the stage where you no longer need to rely on anything, accomplish pure neutrality and dissolve into the vast universe, you are finally free from your desire and will achieve eternal peace.*
- Allow the difficult discussions, but if they blossom into deserving subjects unto themselves, set another meeting to resolve that difficulty.

- Demonstrate sensitivity and tactfulness. Much of this comes from being a good listener, approachable, and laser-focused on the meeting (and project) objectives.
- Use humor wisely. Humor doesn't mean having a witty or ironic office cartoon on every third slide. Humor means saying something funny, witty, insightful, unexpected, and very particular to your location or team—even if you're outrageous or silly once in a while. We have found that it can help a lot, used sparingly, especially in tense moments, with the appropriate acknowledgment of the national and organizational culture in which you use it.
- But be careful that the humor isn't offensive, insensitive, or designed to mock anyone. Once upon a time, that all seemed funny as is demonstrated in a viewing of just about any old movie. But we don't live in that world anymore. Make fun of yourself first or perhaps something about the project or some well-known company quirk.
- Admit that you don't know everything. We're both instructors, and we've come to realize that students *expect* us to know everything. But we don't. And so, while it's tempting to bluff your way through an answer, refrain mightily from doing that. An occasional "I'm not sure, let me get back to you on that" isn't a failure on your part. Rather, it demonstrates that you know what you don't know. Ironically, this is what know-it-alls do not know.
- Watch your (and others') nonverbal communication. It's never good when someone folds their arms across their chest or turns a cold shoulder toward you. Learn to read the signs. If you'd like to use a little humor, tell your attendees that you're an expert at reading body language, and that you, for example, recognize that the forehead on table position indicates that the meeting may have gone on a bit too long. (We have a whole chapter on nonverbal communication.)
- Establish an environment of devil's advocacy. This is particularly important for meetings in which you are reviewing risk. If you are, for example, looking to identify safety risks in your meeting, you do *not* want the introverted analyst who has found something deadly to withdraw into a corner

and hold her thought to herself for fear of being a naysayer. Remind your participants that they are allowed to speak up with such concerns, speaking as a devil's advocate if they choose. For much more on this, note that Chapter 7 addresses this phenomenon. You can also refer to the outstanding book by Jim Detert, *Choosing Courage*, or at least watch this short video: www.youtube.com/watch?v=5h6uqgaGJIc.

All of this guidance is well and good. But is it good enough? What makes meetings, well, *meetings*, is that they're collections of people. And some people, at least sometimes, are monsters.

If you don't believe us, just consider pedestrians and drivers. Guess what? The former turns into the latter as soon as they get in a vehicle. Ask yourself, really ask yourself this question: do you behave exactly the same when you are strolling down the sidewalk, as when you are driving on a Paris roundabout or in heavy New York City traffic?

Both authors are completely willing to admit that they lose their Zen a lot more in a car than they do while walking. And those other drivers? You know, the ones who signal left and turn right, stop without warning, drive at night without any lights on, or have had their left turn indicator blinking since 1978? What do you think about *them*? Guess what? When they get out of their car, they turn back into a pedestrian. So, just like pedestrians turn into drivers, everyday team members turn into meeting attendees. And that isn't always pretty. If you want to see this in action, here is a clip from the Netflix series *Atypical*: https://youtu.be/xYGWka_Rud0.

War Story—Don't Let Humor Bug You— Use It (Carefully)

We (not the authors) met with Secretary of State Madeleine Albright, who told us of the time when the Russian government had bugged the U.S. State Department, a serious breach in international diplomacy. After learning about the bugging, Secretary Albright then went to her next meeting with the Russian foreign minister, wearing a bug pin.

An enormous bug pin. She shared how the foreign minister couldn't help but smile, and she also shared how the energy in the room shifted, and it changed the conversation entirely. This story illuminates at least two things that are true. First, that humor is a choice, one we make in small moments and in big ones, too. And second, that the balance of gravity and levity gives power to both. We can do serious things without taking ourselves so seriously, and in fact, often, we can do them better, and more fashionably.

—Jennifer Aaker and Naomi Bagdonas, who teach "Humor: Serious Business", at Stanford's Graduate School of Business

Meeting the Monsters Head On

As you've seen from the anecdotes in this book, there are all sorts of challenges in facilitating a project meeting. Some come from your physical environment, such as uncontrolled (or just uncomfortable) temperature in the room, faulty imaging, or Internet systems, or local (or very distant) noise such as drilling from a construction project on the floor above you, or a toilet flushing (seemingly forever) from halfway around the world.

But most facilitation challenges originate from the monster-like behavior of human beings—we call them as follows.

Meeting Goblins!

You know them. They interrupt your meeting or derail it. They show up late or start side conversations. They grunt or grumble, they contradict you or others at the meeting, and, in the worst case, they even bully you or other participants. They are often disgruntled and mess things up for those who are eternally gruntled! (Yes, we know there is no such word as gruntled, but your authors are easily amused.)

Please note: we have given names to the goblins to make them seem more real. If you happen to share a name with a goblin, please know that it's a coincidence and nothing personal!

Facilitators need to squelch our built-in propensity to be really nice people when the goblins strike. We need to handle these kinds of behaviors effectively—directly and quickly, even at the risk of insulting or chasing away a goblin. Remember: we're actually opposed to the goblin *behavior*—not the individuals involved. In effect, we're being not nice to the other participants by letting the goblins hijack the meeting. Here are some ways in which you can deal with meeting goblins, and how you can even bring aboard other attendees as allies in the great meeting goblin wars!

Flo the Flow Fouler

Authors' note: we are grateful to the illustrator and innovator Christina Carlson (e-mail: christina@ unstuck.network; website: https://whatsupunstuck.com) whose talents allowed us to bring the meeting goblins to life for our readers! She is also responsible for the book's cover art.

Let's start with the macro disrupters—goblins who arrive too late or too early, make frequent exits and entrances, or are constantly missing meetings. They're disrupting the flow of the meeting, which is why we call them Flow Goblins. In the following scenarios, we'll call this Goblin (what else?) Flo. When meeting attendance is an issue, here are some things you might do:

- Set ground rules about attendance—get a commitment from people that they will attend. Perhaps start your meeting officially at five minutes past the hour, noting that other meetings scheduled to end at the top of the hour often go over. Some companies even customize Outlook and other meeting scheduling software to make these sorts of adjustments automatically.

- If Flo is a habitual latecomer or, if it's a problem, an early arriver, speak to her one-on-one after the meeting. Don't stop the meeting or go back to review something if Flo arrives late. She's late. If you review what she missed, she's making 15 other people late. Ask one of the attendees to catch Flo up after the meeting. Or better yet, do it yourself.
- At the end of the meeting, take a moment to review the upcoming schedule and reconfirm availability.
- Don't be shy about going to Flo's functional (line) manager once you've exhausted the other possibilities. (This is true of all the goblins.) Just state the facts and the effects of Flo's *behavior* on the meetings and the project objectives; don't make it a personal attack.
- This will *not* make Flo love you. But your goal is to meet the objectives of the project, and that is virtually impossible when you have people who do not want to play by the rules of the game.

Guo the Garrulous

Now let's deal with the Garrulous Goblin—we'll call him Guo—who talks too long, or just too much, or in any way that seems to reduce participation by the fuller set of attendees. Here are some tips for addressing issues caused by Guo:

- It's okay to interject, and perhaps rather boisterously, "Thank you, Guo, we hear you. We need to get a wide variety of opinions on this issue." Then, in the same breath, and pointing to one of the quieter participants, say, "Juanita, what do *you* think about this option?"
- Remind Guo, and everyone else, of the agenda and the need to make the most use of your limited time together.
- It's very possible that Guo only wants attention, so don't spend a lot of time giving Guo eye contact. Or use the opposite approach—overdo it. Go right over to Guo and hover. He may—and probably will—back off.
- Write down what Guo said (the main point) on the whiteboard. Guo may then feel that he's literally left his mark on the meeting and give up the floor. Sometimes the guy (or gal) who makes all the noise actually has a valid point.
- Institute a time limit for each person, perhaps two minutes per speaker. Hopefully, this is in your ground rules already, but if it's not, nothing prevents you from improvising.
- Call for a break. Say, "You know what? I'll be sure I capture what Guo says, but (looking at watch), I think it's time for a biological break. See you back here in ten minutes." While you capture what Guo says, address the issue with him (privately and directly) about the effect he's having on the meeting.

NOTE: We made Guo a male for a very specific reason. *Pay attention, men*: According to a George Washington University study (Hancock and Rubin 2015), when men were talking with women, they interrupted them *33 percent more often than when talking with men*. The men interrupted women 2.1 times in a three-minute conversation, dropping to 1.8 times in a male-to-male conversation. Women interrupted men as little as once in a three-minute conversation. This corroborates an older study from Stanford University (Zimmerman and West 1996).

Tina the Tangent Taker

A close cousin of the Garrulous Goblin is the Tangent Goblin. This goblin is either focused on a personal agenda and continues to steer the conversation to her specific point (which is not on-topic) or simply has the habit of going off on tangents that aren't productive for your meeting's objectives. Let's call our Tangent Goblin Tina. How should you address issues caused by Tina?

- Say, "Tina, this is very interesting. Can you tell us how this relates to the risk response options we're discussing?"
- Use the time-limit ideas from the Garrulous Goblin.
- If all else fails, simply be direct. "Tina, we need to get back on schedule. We were discussing risk response options—any other ideas?" (turning your head) "Cathy, didn't you have some ideas on this?"
- Do not make these statements in a tense, angry voice. Always pleasant, always business-like. "This is not the discussion I wanted to have right now."

Billy the Bully

Some attendees are bullies. They may be bullying another attendee or you as a facilitator, or the objectives of the meeting (see the Naysayer Goblin next). If you're unlucky enough to have a Bully Goblin (we'll call him Billy), here's what you can consider doing and saying as a facilitator:

- Step 1: Stop the meeting and have a one-on-one conversation with Billy. Ask what's behind his severe criticism and be sure you express to him that it's coming across as an attack. If it's based on something from outside the meeting (which is likely), request that he leave this baggage out of your project meeting. Ask Billy what the meeting—or the project—could do to address his underlying concern.
- Step 2 (only if Step 1 doesn't work): Call him out. Say, "Billy, I consider what you're doing to be bullying and we cannot tolerate that. Please focus on the issues and stop this behavior. You'll be more likely to make your point in a civil manner."

- When all else fails, you may have to remove him from the meeting. Note that we are often asked what to do if the goblin behavior comes from a superior. Unless you were aware of it premeeting and addressed it with him or her individually, you are going to have to recognize that you may be in a toxic environment. That situation is outside the scope of this book, and you are going to have to deal with that as best you can.

Nadia the Naysayer

You may have a goblin who is constantly negative. Nothing you do is right, nothing works around here, the project has no chance of success, everything is falling apart. We'll call this person the Naysayer Goblin. They may simply always be pessimistic, or they may have the extra attribute of being unnecessarily contradictory. What do you do with Naysayer Nadia?*

---

* Nadia is loosely based on the character created by an actress from the authors' home area of Boston, Rachel Dratch. She created a character called Debbie Downer on *Saturday Night Live*. You can see Debbie (and thus a little of Nadia) here: https://youtu.be/TfE93xON8jk.

- Let's start with the good things that Naysayer Nadia may bring to the meeting. You need a contrary view. You need someone to identify possible flaws in your thinking. So be careful with the other tips here because sometimes—and there's a bit of an art in determining when that time is—Naysayer Nadia is helping you!

- Use a little humor. In one meeting in which one of us had a Naysayer Goblin, he simply said, "You know, Nadia—the pessimists are always *eventually* right. Rome fell, and the dinosaurs went extinct, but they both had a good run. Let's focus on the specific ways in which we can improve this project." That actually muted Naysayer Nadia.

- Challenge Nadia to give three examples of good or successful things about the project.

- Don't let Nadia give out a laundry list of all that's wrong with the project. After she's dropped a couple of negatives on the meeting, say "Okay, Nadia, can you stop right there and give us some suggestions on how we can fix those first two problems?"

Passive-Aggressive Pat

According to the Mayo Clinic: Passive–aggressive behavior is a pattern of indirectly expressing negative feelings instead of openly addressing them. There's a disconnect between what a person who exhibits passive–aggressive behavior says and what he or she does.

For example, someone who engages in passive–aggressive behavior might appear to agree—perhaps even enthusiastically—with another person's request. Rather than complying with the request, however, he or she might express anger or resentment by failing to follow through or missing deadlines.

The problem with this type of behavior is not only that it can be difficult to deal with, but it can also be difficult to *diagnose* or figure out if the person really is passive–aggressive, disorganized, or just not up to the job.

War Story: One of us managed a program for a large virtual private network (VPN) rollout for a telecommunications company. His job as project manager was to pull all the various pieces (cybersecurity, software and hardware, tech writing, etc.) together to create a schedule. He had had a lot of trouble getting dates from the software manager. So, they arranged to meet in the manager's office at 2 p.m. one afternoon.

When our naïve, intrepid PM went to the office on the stated date and time, the door was closed, and the software manager had left for the day. Subsequently, our author had no choice but to go to the boss and report. She tracked the manager down and got what we needed. However, from that point on, there was some friction between the two. But *c'est la vie*. Again, if you want everyone to like you, find another profession. To a large extent, project management involves getting people to take their medicine whether they want to or not.

According to a *Harvard Business Review* study, the cost of passive–aggressiveness is high. At the business level, the negative effects include slow decision making, poor risk identification and mitigation, and stalled execution. On the team level, unarticulated but apparent frustrations erode trust, interfere with communication, and contribute to animosity. For individuals, the prolonged stress of unaddressed conflict takes a toll. Everyone suffers.

Passive–aggressive behavior might manifest itself in a meeting by sarcasm, eye-rolling, caustic *jokes*, the silent treatment, consistent late arrival at meetings, not following through on actions. Remember—this is a certain amount of hostility expressed passively. You can see some great examples in this helpful video (https://youtu.be/Sm6NCwyBrqg).

In order to have the ability to run your meeting, you will have no choice but to derail the behavior. You cannot call it out directly for what it is—you are a PM, not a psychologist. But you can address it firstly by calling the individual aside privately and asking what's preventing them from meeting deadlines or if there is some issue with the project. Or even, for that matter, an issue with you.

Sidebar Sal

Some folks can't help having side conversations with their neighbor, and this can be annoying and disruptive. We'll call this the Sidebar Goblin, and we'll call him Sal. It's no coincidence that you may recognize some of the corrections for Sidebar Sal from your middle-school English teacher, the one with the tweed jacket with patches on the elbows.

- Say "Sal—I see you have something to say, would you mind sharing it with the entire group?"

- Just stop talking and let silence (or rather residual conversation) do your work. Most people will end up glaring at the people having the side conversation.
- Tap the table (or maybe pound it!) and say, "We need to have one meeting here!"
- Walk over to Sal and his conversation partner (who is probably going to be relieved that you're freeing her from Sal's speech). Your close presence will probably be enough.
- Reiterate the ground rules, which, hopefully, discourage side conversations.
- Remember—people will respect you for keeping the meeting on track. In fact, they'll be looking (literally) at you to do that. If you don't, they'll lose respect for you.
  "How was the meeting?"

"Not so great. Bob couldn't seem to control it and we never got to the full agenda."

"Good to know. I'll try to avoid his meetings. Thanks for the tip."

Rosie the Reticent

Some of your best ideas, opportunities, threats, comments, and other gems reside in the minds of your most quiet, introverted people. Just as a business analyst must elicit requirements from clients, you may have to apply those skills to elicit these gems in meetings.

Some of the most striking examples of disastrous projects could have been averted (think Space Shuttle Discovery, the Dieselgate scandal of VW, the Boeing 737 Max 8 launch) if important concerns had been voiced, whether in or outside of a meeting. Don't be the facilitator that squelched an important voice—or created an environment that was focused on agreement and stifled the ability to speak up with a valid objection. See our chapter on this topic, mysteriously entitled *Deviled Eggs*.

How to get Rosie to speak up?

- Be sure that the ground rules regarding a safe environment are clear to everyone—those that may make it uncomfortable for Rosie—and Rosie herself.
- Remind her of how important her input is, use disastrous examples if necessary—and point out that she can help prevent them.
- Demonstrate the behavior of recognizing the more introverted participants when they do speak up.
- It may take a more customized approach; having knowledge about a particular Rosie—interests within and outside of work, for example—can be a conversation starter outside the meeting to ease a path forward for talking with you.
- Here's a tip that works—elicit their input casually before the meeting, acknowledge their ideas or concerns, and let them know they're important (by *they*, we mean the ideas and the person), and that you may be discussing this at the upcoming meeting. At the meeting, say, "Actually, Rosie brought up a very good idea... Rosie—would you mind summarizing the discussion we had the other day?" This works wonders.

Sandeep the Showboat

To be a showboat—derived from its original meaning of a river steamboat on which theatrical performances are given—means to show off and be dramatically expressive for no other reason than to get attention. We like this definition: *ostentatious behavior that is apparently designed to attract attention and admiration* (Macmillan Dictionary). Think of an athlete doing a celebratory dance (for way too long, and very poorly) after scoring a goal, basket, or touchdown. "Hey, everybody, look at ME!" is the tagline of this goblin.

In meetings, Sandeep the Showboat will try to dominate the meeting, speak at length about the one or two things about which he's (allegedly) knowledgeable, and even things he's not, and do it for the love of the spotlight more than wanting to contribute. In fact, with goblins like Reticent Rosie around, he's doing the opposite of contributing—he's preventing others from contributing. Other participants are saying to themselves, "Well, if the facilitator is letting Sandeep go on and on, I'm tuning out."

Off they go to Expedia.com to shop around for that perfect vacation spot for their long-overdue postpandemic getaway. You probably notice that Sandeep's behavior is similar to that of Guo the Garrulous.

That means you can refer to the solutions for that goblin and apply them to Sandeep. The difference is that Guo is going on because he likes to talk. Sandeep wants attention and would like to (and we've actually seen this attempted) go right up to the front of the meeting room, grab the marker from you (or the Zoom equivalent, start sharing his screen), and take over the meeting. Do not let this happen! (Please go to the whiteboard right now and write down 100 times "I will not let my meeting be hijacked.")

- Be sure you have set the ground rules and remind Sandeep that he's agreed to them.
- Let him have the spotlight by promising him an even *brighter* one: Invite him to host his very own meeting on a particular project threat or focus area, and the show is all his. Then, let him settle back in his seat, where he will likely fantasize about his upcoming stardom, and you can get back to facilitating your meeting.

We'll leave this chapter with one final tip: Sometimes in meetings you're a problem-solver, and that means that you need to understand the causes of the problems and not just the symptoms. Admittedly, your attendees aren't six-year-old problem children on an airplane, but the poem next, which features a six-year-old problem child, goes a long way in explaining how you may have to think to reconcile troublesome meeting attendees.

A gentleman traveling on a coast-to-coast flight
Was the kind of a person who had real insight.
A six-year-old youngster was really a fright
Running up and down aisles and giving a fight.
The people in business were trying to work
Near those who were sleeping, the youngster did lurk.
He yanked off the headsets of some music lovers,
And took all of the peanuts that he could discover.

The passengers complained, "He must be controlled."
And threatened the flight crew to knock him out cold.

The flight attendant buckled him into his seat
But his screams and his hollers were less than a treat.

The passengers, desperate, want him bound tight and gagged.
"Arrest the boy's parents or let them be nagged."
At last, comes our gentleman, who spoke to the crew.
They loved his idea; into action they flew.

They found a seat for the boy in the front of the plane.
They were willing to do it to keep themselves sane.
They fashioned a steering wheel from a large plate.
A stick was a rudder; he thought it was great.

Flying instruments were made from some odds and some ends.
The pilot came back; the two became friends.
The pilot then asked for help flying the plane
Because it'd be tough if they ran into rain.

The kid was delighted; he was taught how to fly.
Flight attendants all smiled; the copilot came by.
The pilot saluted and left the boy in command.
He kept pretty quiet and thought it was grand.

The passengers rejoiced; the gentleman was praised.
"How did you think of it?" the question was raised.
The gentleman answered in a voice calm and low,
"It's really quite simple if you go with the flow.
You tried hard to solve your own problem, the noise.
But the problem I solved was that of the boy's."

—Janice Y. Preston, CPA, PMP

Summary

The bottom line is that sometimes people come to a meeting with an agenda, and it's not *your* agenda. It's a *hidden* agenda. Often people feel that, in life or in their job, they're not being heard. Maybe they've witnessed project after project fail, and they want to be sure that you understand this. Let them be heard but let them know that their ideas must be expressed in a constructive manner.

That's a quick summary of ways to improve the facilitation of your meeting. We're sure it can help you now. And Zen. (Apologies to Robert Plant.)

References

Hancock, A.B. and B.A. Rubin. 2015. *Influence of Communication Partner's Gender on Language.* sagepub.com.

https://hbr.org/2016/01/reduce-passive-aggressive-behavior-on-your-team.

Zimmerman, D.H. and C. West 1996. *Sex Roles, Interruptions and Silences in Conversation.* zimmermanwest1975.pdf (stanford.edu).

CHAPTER 5

Nonverbal Communications and Body Language

Key Takeaways

- 🗪 Communication, perhaps especially in meetings, is about much more than words.
- 🗪 Becoming a good meeting facilitator, and in fact, a good project leader, requires knowledge of nonverbal communication, including body language, facial expressions, paralinguals, and even seating arrangements.
- 🗪 We provide pointers for these nonverbal forms of communications, focused on project meetings.

Disclaimer

There is, we believe, good advice in this chapter; however, don't take every crossing of the arms or shifting in the seat as any particular pointed message. We must stress that in some cultures, body language, which is built in to a person's upbringing, will show up and could be giving off signals that you'll improperly interpret. Nothing beats asking someone directly and empathetically how they feel if you sense this form of body language miscommunication.

Communication—It's Not Only About Words!

Consider this statement: "We are never not communicating." Really. Stop reading and say that out loud, pause, and consider what that means.

The idea behind this statement is that even when you don't intend to, you are sending messages. Behavioral analysis provides us great insights into the ways that we may be (intentionally or otherwise) communicating with others in meetings, thanks to our body language and other nonverbal ways we show up in meetings.

Why does this matter? Because in the post-COVID-19 era, we have more meetings than ever. So, let's highlight some insights into nondirect, perhaps unintentional, meeting communications that are important to our roles as project leaders and understand how we might leverage them to help productivity in our meetings. This help comes in two forms: (1) it increases our ability to understand others' nonverbal messages and (2) it hones our own skills as leaders to avoid miscommunicating nonverbally.

First, it is important to understand that everyone communicates in multiple ways. We can think of these ways as communications *aspects*—different features or ways of appearing. The three aspects we'll discuss here are: attitude, nonverbal, and background.

The attitude aspect: Attitude is an excellent aspect for us to leverage. Often, attitude toward any given topic forms the basis of nonverbal responses. A great mistake is to think about attitude in isolation of your meeting. Yes, it's well known that a poor attitude toward a discussion topic of your meeting may show itself as body language that is very standoffish and disconnected. However, it could also mean that the person could have had some other previous bad experience and the attitude observed in the body language is residual from that. They could also just be having a bad day.

It is also important to understand that attitude is composed of emotional and behavioral responses in both cases. Watching the attitude aspect, project leaders can understand which team members we might need to check in with during or after our meeting. Projects are a team sport. We, as project leaders, need to do everything in our power to help all our team members participate at their highest level of performance. Meetings—for an observant facilitator—provide an excellent opportunity to detect and coach based on the attitude aspect.

The nonverbal aspect: There is disagreement about the percentage of communications that is nonverbal. Our findings from conversations with colleague project leaders, combined with our decades of experience tells us that *at least* 50 percent of information exchanged among people can be characterized as such. The nonverbal aspect gives us additional insight about a message from a participant in our meeting—is what we are hearing and seeing matched up with the words? Is there information being conveyed that involves no words at all and instead involves a tone of voice, a wrinkle of the nose, a gesture of the hand (or foot!), or even absence or presence from a meeting?

Thinking about verbal and nonverbal communication *in isolation* could be a missed opportunity. For example, seeing someone shift in their chair or look away during a conversation is meaningless if not taken in context of what is said. Importantly, there is no unique nonverbal behavior exclusively associated with anything. Instead, we must appreciate that our best answers to leveraging nondirect meeting communication are more about active attention—being aware of our attendees' participation.

For understanding nonverbal communication, it is more important to pay attention to each participant within the scope of the meeting and be aware of changes that may occur during the meeting.

We must be aware that participants in our session will also be influenced by our presence *and* the way we show up with our own nonverbal aspect. Suppose we show up with erratic behavior or otherwise fail to inspire safety, inclusiveness, and welcoming energy for all to engage. In that case, we may unknowingly trigger nonverbal responses in others that are irrelevant to the topic at hand because, in fact, they are a response to us.

The background aspect: This is something unique to virtual meetings, which are often accused of being too formal or mechanical. This aspect has been more prominent in the era of meetings since the COVID-19 pandemic.

We often hold video-conferencing meetings (e.g., Zoom, Teams) equally or more than in-person meetings. What people are displaying behind themselves—whether actual camera images, or *fake* backgrounds—affords insights into what might be important or relatable to them. What if they have a Yoda figure or a poster of some musical group (*I love KISS!*) or movie behind them? Not unlike noticing what *totems* people have on their desks at work (the old paradigm), these sources provide you as a project leader with additional routes to access the human behind the sterile role of meeting participant.

For decades, it has been said that people remember how you make them feel more than what you tell them. You want to create a reputation where people enjoy your meetings, which helps them show up at their best. The background aspect can help contribute to your goal.

As with any worthwhile knowledge, it's great to have it, but it's much better if you put it to work. This means being attentive to this knowledge when we are engaging with members of our project team and stakeholders of our projects.

It's also good to note that having a better understanding of nonverbal communication provides you with extra energy, which is contagious to those around us. In this case, let the contagion continue!

Body Language

One of the advantages we've somewhat lost in moving to a virtual world is the ability to read body language. One definition *(Psychology Today)* says this, "Body language is a silent orchestra, as people constantly give clues to what they're thinking and feeling. Nonverbal messages including body movements, facial expressions, vocal tone and volume, and other signals are collectively known as body language."

We assert that it would be wise for you to read this chapter, and start paying closer attention to your attendees' body language.

> Caveat—Freud famously said that *sometimes a cigar is just a cigar.* If someone's taking on what seems to be a defensive posture, maybe they're just cold/tired or late for a show. Use body language as part of your bag of tricks, but don't rely on it exclusively. And unless you're an expert, don't let it override your common sense.

Let's look at some of the more common postures and quirks:

- Folded arms—Folding arms across one's body may mean that they are either uncomfortable with what's being said or perhaps even resistant. It might also occur during stressful conversations. In any event, it is important to find out what's bothering the person. We don't think it's necessary to say something like,

"Hey, Haoyu. I noticed you folded your arms across your chest. Is something bothering you?" At that point, you sound like an (annoying) armchair psychologist. Best to poll a few people and see how they feel about the proposed idea or whatever's causing the grief. Then ask Haoyu directly what he thinks. You may have to coax him out a little bit. If he's reluctant to answer in the session, you may need to talk to him one-on-one.

- Nail biting—If someone is biting their nails or for that matter, putting something in their mouth like a pen, this could indicate nervousness or anxiety.
- Turning away or the cold shoulder—This is a sign of disagreement or, again, shutting someone out. It could also be a signal of frustration.
- Eye movements—It's been commonly believed that when people look down, they're lying, or if they look up, they're trying to remember something. Or perhaps it's the reverse. Nevertheless, it doesn't matter. Contrary to popular belief, there is no scientific evidence to support either of these cases.
- Foot withdrawal—If you ask a question in the meeting and someone pulls their feet back in and crosses them in reaction—that could indicate that the question has made them nervous—but they may instead just have long legs and are rearranging them for their comfort. Make a note of this and approach this person after the meeting, Ask them about that same topic and if there is anything you can do to assure them about the issue at hand—or rather, at foot. Hands being pulled further in (toward the person) may similarly indicate displeasure or nervousness about a topic.
- Mixed messages—The classic example is someone who says, *Yes* but shakes their head *No*. They likely mean *No* but may be having a hard time saying it. The authors' observation is that the average person is nonconfrontational and will do anything to avoid it even if something as innocuous as where to go for lunch. ("No. Really. Wherever YOU want to go.") And for whatever reason, people just hate to say *no* and will do anything to avoid saying it.

Note—Be careful of this. In his book, *Understanding Body Language: How to Decode Nonverbal Communication in Life, Love and Work*, author Scott Rouse relates a story about cross-cultural communication. In a discussion with a woman and her business partner, she had been nodding her head *Yes*, but her words said *No*. It took this body language expert a while to figure out that that's what they do in Bulgaria.

And when he gave her Greek colleague a thumbs up, he almost got into a fight because that otherwise harmless gesture was an insult in parts of Greece.

So, the moral of the story is beware of hand gestures and know the culture of the people you're dealing with.

Facial Expressions

Body language expert and former *spy catcher* Joe Navarro describes the importance of information conveyed by the human face in his books and videos. Vanessa van Edwards, another expert in this area, also has valuable coverage of facial expressions.* We digest a few key tips on reading faces here—with the same caveat as above.

Think of the face in terms of comfort and discomfort. One of the brain's main jobs, after all, is avoiding discomfort and maximizing comfort. And this expresses itself in facial expressions. When in psychological comfort, the face muscles are relaxed, and the pupils are typically slightly wider. The lips are not compressed, and the chin is slightly forward and up.

When psychological discomfort is felt, there will often be furrowing of eyebrows and/or wrinkles appearing at the forehead. The chin may get tucked down and may even slightly vibrate in extreme situations. Often, this psychological discomfort is accompanied by a gesture of the hand to the face, either covering the eyes or shielding of one direction of vision by the hand.

---

* Reference video https://youtu.be/0MtsXbTJdt8 (40-minute Talks at Google, Vanessa van Edwards—covers gestures and details on facial expressions).

One area to which you may pay some attention is the glabella—the area between the eyebrows. When this is wrinkled (and this usually comes along with a brief squint), it indicates discomfort—which, in a meeting context, could indicate confusion, distaste, or even distrust. Your attendees won't tell you what is causing this or whether it even has anything to do with the meeting (they could've just recalled they left the oven on!).

It's your job as a meeting facilitator to note that there is discomfort and check in with the attendee. And if a bunch of attendees are simultaneously reacting in this way—well, our guess is that you have just (for example) said that the meeting is going to go on for another hour or stated a project objective incorrectly. Don't let this slide! If you get that reaction from multiple participants, you should take it just as if they all said out loud, "no that's wrong!," and ask (out loud) if there is a problem of some kind. "Seems like the vibe in the room has changed. What's going on?"

Other Indicators

The nose can convey nonverbals—a *bunny nose*—wrinkling near the nostrils or other indication of a scrunched-up nose—is an expression that can start at ages as young as three months to indicate distaste.

Smiles of various types can be telling. In Navarro's videos, he gives visual examples of a social smile, an interested smile, a curious smile.

Posture, Paralinguals, and Pace

One thing you should be aware of as a facilitator is that you are communicating with body language, even when you walk into a room. Walking smoothly, looking broadly around the room (not down), making eye contact with everyone in the room, and giving a knowing smile—all of these things telegraph confidence. Taking a moment before speaking to get your thoughts together and then owning the room, this conveys confidence. Smooth, easy movements, a lack of fidgeting—these transmit confidence. Compare the self-assured attitude of Glinda the Good Witch to the Cowardly Lion's fidgeting, nervous demeanor in *The Wizard of Oz.*

Confidence is exactly what you want to project—because you are leading the meeting (and the project), people are expecting you to be confident. They're on this project with you and they want to know that you understand it, that you believe in it, and that you believe in yourself. Any signals you give that raise this assessment of confidence will increase your effectiveness as a meeting and project leader. Navarro uses Colin Powell as an example. He walked into the room as a statesman, with everyone knowing that here was a gentleman with a significant amount of knowledge and experience. Seek to channel that behavior when you lead a meeting.

As to paralinguals[†]—avoid uptalk. Uptalk is that (bad) habit of ending very sentence or statement with a rising question-like tone. It gives the impression that you are *guessing* what you are saying rather than making a declarative sentence. Sure, use that rising tone when you are asking the attendees a question: "Karim, you are our expert on servers, do you want to give us your opinion now?" But when Karim agrees to take on the action, you declare, "thanks for doing that, Karim—let's move on to the next item." Note that it does not require talking loudly or saying that you are in charge. It's often quiet confidence that conveys the message most strongly.

Another interesting point made by Navarro is the idea of being in charge of time. By that, we don't mean assuring that agenda items don't go over their allotted time (although that's important as well). Instead, it is about answering questions at your pace, not rushing them, not letting others take the pace of the meeting in their own hands. You may need to be more commanding than usual, but you are indeed there to act as a project and meeting leader, and that means that you set the pace.

Macro Body Language

We've discussed ways you communicate with your face and body with mostly subtle, micro movements of the eyes, mouth, hands, arms, and so on.

[†] Paralinguals are properties of speech, such as speaking tempo, vocal pitch, and intonational contours, which can be used to communicate attitudes or other shades of meaning in addition to (or in conflict with!) the actual words being used.

NONVERBAL COMMUNICATIONS AND BODY LANGUAGE   63

There's one more thing to discuss—moving your *whole* body (think back to the *hokey-pokey; you put your whole self in, you put your whole self out...*). In the extreme case, attendees may simply *not* arrive at a meeting, or arrive late, or leave early. That indeed is body language: macro body language.

As a convener and facilitator of meetings, you certainly need to pay attention to this. Returning to the key message from this chapter, we are never *not* communicating, so that person leaving early or arriving late could be indicating that they are not on board with the project. But as we also mentioned that "a cigar is sometimes just a cigar," so perhaps they have an ongoing conflict. It's your job to find out. You should be unshy about asking people if there is something keeping them from attending your whole meeting. Or for that matter, being wholly present. Based on their response, make an informed agenda redesign.

To underline the caveat we made earlier about using only snippets of body language—out of context—to make judgments, we share with you this real project war story.

I was the latest in a series of senior project directors of a telecom project that had been going on for several years, in a remote location of the United States. As the vendor, we were responsible for deploying the network, the customer had obligations to prepare sites to be ready for equipment and services.

I grew up and went to school in Italy. The customer was Italian, and my counterpart project manager (PM) was (like me) an engineer who had become a PM. The two of us had established a working relationship during the past year that enabled the project to steadily move forward, albeit slowly.

A newly formed small team in the corporate headquarters sent, without notifying me, a business expert to assess the progress of this project. The expert arrived while I was on a short vacation. She interviewed the project team, then asked to join our weekly project meeting with the customer, whom she had never met.

At the end of the meeting, back at our office, we had a follow-up meeting in which the business expert revealed with the utmost confidence her clear understanding of my customer PM counterpart's feelings and intentions, which she had gained by her keen observation of his body language. Her conclusion was that our customer PM was feeling betrayed by our company, as we had not delivered what had been promised, and that the customer PM was convinced of the strength of his own team, which was doing what was needed to secure project completion. I listened politely and shared my interpretation of the *unspoken* part of the meeting, which was quite different from hers.

In my opinion, the customer PM was very dissatisfied with his current career outlook and the relocation he had to accept to lead this project, which was, to him, a source of frustration due to the ineptitude of some members of his team. My insights were based on having worked with the PM for over a year, learning his *modus operandi* and his thinking patterns, and observing his reactions to project roadblocks and delays, not by a two-hour meeting, not by interpreting his body language—not by analyzing silent communications out of context, that could mean so many different things, based on geographical, organizational, and personal culture.

As it turned out, we learned the following week that the customer's project team had spectacularly failed in its obligations to install equipment needed for us (the vendor) to configure the network, and my PM counterpart left his company two weeks later for a better job elsewhere.

—Anonymous (from a global project
director of major telecom deployments)

Story anonymous at author's request

Another form of macro body language, more applicable to formal meetings, is seating. Where you sit in a meeting makes a difference (Figure 5.1). This is truer in some places than others. (That said, sitting at the head of the table has pretty much the same meaning worldwide.) In Japan, for example, there are names for certain seats. The seat farthest

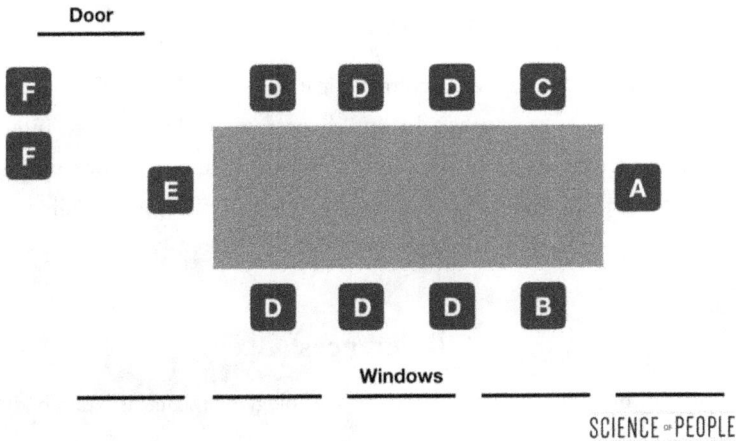

Figure 5.1 Meeting seating is important
Source: www.scienceofpeople.com/seating-arrangement/.

from and facing the door is called *kamiza* (上座) and is reserved for the most senior individual at the meeting.

The seat closest to the door is called *shimoza* (下座) and usually indicates the person most junior in your team. This long-held practice arises from the understanding that the seat farthest from the door is the calmest and less exposed to foot traffic and interruption by subordinates.

In more general terms, here are some tips, drawn from an outstanding resource called "The Science of People."

In this setup, A is the power position. B and C are the allies. Seats marked *D* are the middles and would have to lean forward or raise their hands (and should!) if they want attention. Position *E* is called the contender, and the person sitting there is holding a potentially contrary position (physically). If you are sitting in a contender seat and are in alignment with the leader (at seat A), you may need to show more supportive verbal and body language. For people who are going to need to enter/exit quickly, seat positions F makes the most sense. Note that there is an important dynamic in meetings, which include customers, which is not included in this brief section. Recognizing that this could be another entire book, we instead provide you with references on that dynamic.

Summary

Understand that we are always communicating—and that we do so often without the use of any words. In this chapter, we review ways to interpret those nonverbal communications and provide resources for a deeper dive into the fascinating world of human communication, especially in a group setting—like a project team meeting.

References

Definition of Body language: www.psychologytoday.com/us/basics/body-language.

More details about seating arrangements at meetings here: www.scienceofpeople .com/seating-arrangement/.

If you really want to get into the weeds on body language in general, check out the four experts on the Behavior Panel. (Scott Rouse, whose book is mentioned above, is one of the four experts. These guys analyze people who are in the news, going into great detail on their facial body language.) www.youtube.com/c/TheBehaviorPanel.

CHAPTER 6

The Importance of Team Building

Key Takeaways

- Teams are how project work is done. Building teams is what project leaders do. And project meetings are where great teams are built and strengthened.
- A team is much more than a collection of individuals. A team has cohesiveness.
- Agile-based teams have some additional characteristics, which we review.
- Diversity in teams has both contributory and detrimental aspects to cohesion. We provide advice as to how to maximize the former and minimize the latter.
- There are specific ideas for breaking the ice to assist in team formation.
- There is science behind team formation, using the Tuckman and Gersick models, with an important tangent on conflict resolution, using the Thomas–Kilmann conflict mode instrument.

A great slugger we haven't got...
A great pitcher we haven't got...
A great ball club we haven't got ...
What've we got? We've got heart! All you really need is heart.
When the odds are sayin' you'll never win, that's when the grins should start

—"Heart," from the 1955 musical, *Damn Yankees.*
By Richard Adler and Jerry Ross.

To convince you how important this topic is to projects, have another glimpse at the title of our book. Yep, teams is right there in the title. So, it is incumbent upon us to discuss project teams, the great and the not-so-great. We believe firmly that great meetings build great teams. But meetings are not the *only* way to build them.

In project management—as in sports—there's nothing more important, more fundamental than the team. Consider sports teams for a moment. If all that mattered in professional sports was having the best talent, then the team with the highest payroll would always win. But that's not always the case. Often the team that wins is the one that wants it most, that is the best-managed, and that takes whatever level of player is there—some superstars, some not—and blends them into a whole greater than the sum of its parts. You've gotta have heart!

To quote a recent article in the *Harvard Business Review*:

A useful way to think about teams with the right mix of skills and personalities is to consider the two roles every person plays in a working group: a *functional* role, based on their formal position and technical skill, and a *psychological* role, based on the kind of person they are. Too often, organizations focus merely on the functional role and hope that good team performance somehow follows. This is why even the most expensive professional sports teams often fail to perform according to the individual talents of each player: There is no psychological synergy.

A team that works together tends to get more done, faster, and better than a team that doesn't. After all, a project manager's charge is to get work done through others—and most of those others function as your core project team. You are the leader of a temporary team. But you can't expect to bring a group of individuals together, however well they may know each other, and have a team automatically form. The process takes care and feeding, and by that, we mean that you need to become more informed about how teams are built, and once you get there, you can be the *nurturer* of your project teams.

We came across the following graphic and liked it (Figure 6.1). And while it refers to employees, there is no reason you cannot substitute the expression 'team members' there just as well. And while it is not specific to Agile, there certainly is an element of servant leadership.

So, before we talk about team building, what does this semimythical beast, the oft heard of but less often witnessed well-run, well-oiled team look like? And is this ideal different when we go from waterfall to Agile?

Let's look first at the idea of the well-run, cohesive team in general. The authors' observation is that it has a number of attributes. The team:

- Gets along well on a personal level.
- Understands and respects each other in terms of need for space, professional ability, accountability, and working together.

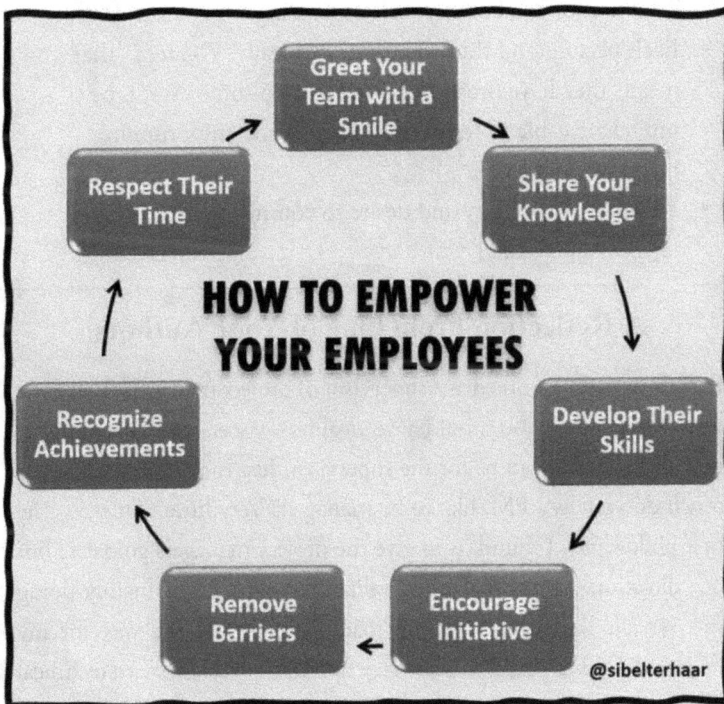

Figure 6.1 The well-oiled team—your authors' view
Graphic courtesy of Sibel Terhaar.

- Supports each other. If one person can't handle something perhaps due to overload or time pressure, another team member can sense this and asks how they can help. (Agilists sometimes swarm to get a particular task done. Swarming means they all work on one task together.)
- Gets results. But they get those results without burning bridges or burning out.
- Has good, fair leadership, command and control, or servant–leader style, as appropriate for the methodology and situation.
- Has a clear sense of its mission.
- Has high team morale and team identification.
- Overall: has a high level of cohesion or unity.

The preceding elements are true whether the team is waterfall or Agile based. But we would add these attributes for Agile teams:

- They are (or can become) self-organizing.
- Each person (and thus the team) is, ideally, *T-shaped*. That means they have broad skills and can, to some extent, be interchangeable in terms of skillsets, leadership, running meetings, and so on.
- They have the ability and desire to commit to each other.

A Reflection From One of Your Authors

For many years, I worked as a supervisor of project managers. If you are a project manager, you should have an almost visceral understanding of how difficult that can be for the supervisor. Just turn it around—how much do you, as a PM, like to be managed? Very little, I'm sure. The best philosophy, I found, is to give the project managers guidance but not direction. In a way, I now realize that what I was mainly doing was servant leadership—getting roadblocks out of the way for my PMs, letting them excel at what they did best—working with technical teams (designers, product managers, installation and testing groups, and telecom customers) to bring up service on telecom networks.

Of all of the groups of project managers I worked with, the best—by far—was one that was wildly diverse in terms of background, age, gender, and ethnicity. There was more energy, creativity, and just plain old success, in this team as compared to others. It was also the scenario in which I learned the most about teamwork, about project leadership, and about personal dynamics.

This situation may even explain why I stuck with project management as a career—the chance to work with diverse teams all the time. Project managers have to assemble outcome-focused teams from across functional and geographical areas. So, in an odd way, each project manager is building teams that ideally behave like that great group I was proud to work with in my career.

Team-Building Methods

In our travels, we've discovered that many project managers take an all-or-nothing approach to team building. "We can't afford to send the team off to Outward Bound or some other offsite retreat," they'll say, "So we won't do *anything*." Who says you have to give up on team building because you can't take the team on an outing?

You can build the team in other ways. One of us recently joined a project where the team was 100 percent virtual. The product owner asked us to team up in pairs, interview each other, and create mind maps that would detail interesting facts about the other person. We then presented those on-screen in our meeting and got to know people on a personal level. We found that this helped facilitate the getting to know you part, which in turn helped us work together better on the project. (You are forgiven if you broke out into a version of "Getting to Know You, Getting to Know All About You" just now.)

If you'd like to accelerate the process of team members getting to know each other with a quick and easy-to-implement exercise, we suggest Human Bingo. The use of this game will depend on the culture of your organization, but we've used it at conservative banks and energy firms with success. The steps are easy:

- Create bingo cards (5 × 5 square grid) and make sufficient copies for everyone.
- Customize the card to stimulate conversation by filling in the boxes with humorous and/or mildly controversial (or at least interesting) traits or characteristics (see Figure 6.2).
- Give each attendee a card and a pen or pencil.
- Explain the rules:
  - Each person is to go around the room, introduce them-selves (name only) and either offer up a square or seek one from another player. When people pair up like this, the intent is that they each give the other one square.
  - A square is attained by having the other individual write their name or initials on a square that accurately describes them—for example, "I am left-handed." Then the roles are reversed—each person walks away from the transaction with one, and only one, square signed by the other person. Each transaction should only last a few minutes.
  - Players continue to circulate, seeking a row (or rows) of signed squares (bingo!), or, depending on the amount of time, as many signed squares as they can get.
  - Call time and end the exercise. For a group of 20 people, typically you can call time after 20 to 25 minutes.
- Declare the winner. Do a readout at the end by asking who made a bingo (horizontal, vertical, diagonal). Several people will usually have at least one bingo. If no one has a bingo, you can ask, "Who has more than ten squares signed?" and ask people to leave their hands up as you ask, "More than eleven?," "More than twelve?," and so on. The last person with their hand up is the winner. You can decide whether to have a token prize for the top performers.

This exercise usually provides not only a chance for team members to meet each other but also tends to bring a lot of positive energy (and fun) to the meeting.

B	I	N	G	O
I have tasted Xibei (西北) cuisine (or at least... know what it is)	I am afraid of heights	My undergrad degree was "technical"	I have been on a brewery tour	Sometimes I eat dessert first (and after) a meal
I have a pet at home	I live within 10 miles of the office	I am a soccer fan	I am good at technical things	I consider myself a bit of a wine connoisseur (Okay, okay, a _snob_)
I have visited Prague, (Czech Rep.)	I was born in the same month as you	Free Square	I play an instrument (Not necessarily a virtuoso!)	I am an only child
I speak a language other than English	I've been to at least 2 baseball parks	I admit it: I almost always "jaywalk" or cross the street when the red hand is up	I was on a subway within the past 3 months	I am at least 'average' at playing tennis
I am a "night owl" – (I stay up late)	I am a member of the Project Management Institute (PMI®)	I have a nickname (you don't have to share it, just admit you have one if you do)	I have run in a competitive long-distance race	I had some University courses outside of (region)

Figure 6.2 Example of a Human Bingo card

In addition to the Human Bingo exercise, your team-building budget might be able to cover fun activities such as bowling or some other sporting event. Escape rooms—where the team works to find a way out of a room within an hour—are a fun way to build a team (see Figure 6.3).

Even if the team isn't working together toward a common goal, it's in these informal situations where the pictures of the kids come out or people talk about their pets—and they become a lot more open to relationship building.

Be sure that whatever your team-building event is, it is something everyone wants to do. One of us was involved in a paintball team-building exercise. This actually worked well as the teams were dysfunctional, and they worked toward a common goal. But it also wound up excluding a number of people who thought it was too violent or wouldn't be fun.

And lastly, working together in the facilitated meeting is a great way to build a team. Yes, there will be arguments, clashes, and conflicts of

Figure 6.3 A group of happy co-workers enjoying their escape room success[*]

Photo used by permission of Boxaroo. Puzzle and Escape Room Adventures, Boston, MA.

opinion during the session. But these are, or should be, healthy discussions, not negative interactions. It's the job of the facilitator and sponsor to keep conflict focused on the problem and not the people.

Team-building examples—what *not* to do—another story from the authors' files.

War Story—Good Intentions Aren't Enough!

Sometimes the best intentions don't lead to the best outcomes. Consider the experience of one of the authors. He was consulting to a financial institution and was invited to a team-building event. The company was headquartered in Boston but had satellite offices in other parts of the country.

---

[*] Actually this is one of the authors' daughters.' From left to right, Jesse Dalton, Pam Rerko Dalton, Jessica Stewart, and the ringleader, Kathleen Hong.

Prior to the event, we were asked to submit a list of accomplishments both personal and professional. We were also advised we were going to play a game called *Two Truths and a Lie*. If you're not familiar with it, you offer up two true things about yourself, and one totally made up fact. It's used not only as an icebreaker but also as a way to gauge how well the attendees are getting to know each other.

So, on the appointed day, we all met at the HQ in Boston. There were approximately 20 people, or enough to fit around a good-sized conference table.

The first problem to note was that on one side of the room was a screen, which was scrolling all our accomplishments. Which nobody could or did read. The list just scrolled endlessly while we chatted. A lost opportunity.

The second problem came when we introduced ourselves. Here, we thought, was a chance to start to get to know people. But the introductions went like this—"Mary Jones, San Diego, Operations," "Morton Nzuka, Boston, Sales," and so on. All the way down the line. Name, rank, serial number. One hour into the meeting, and we knew exactly as much about each other as we did when we walked in.

Then after a while, a manager from another division popped in and advised the entire group (to the chagrin of our manager) that there was going to be a haircut. That was company slang for layoff. So, needless to say, that statement dampened our enthusiasm a bit.

We then went to another room, got into groups, and played *Two Truths and a Lie*. Now, as the author knew nothing about his colleagues, one guess was as good as another. So, if someone told him they studied to be an astronaut, opened up an ice cream shop, and played the ukulele, there was really no way to know the truth from the lie.

We then later walked to another building owned by the company where they kept newspaper headlines up on the wall about the history of the company. Fascinating in its own way one supposes, but it turns out that craning your neck to look up at a wall doesn't encourage interaction.

The final event was dinner at a very long table at a restaurant in Boston where one could only speak (without shouting) to the person next to you who you may already have worked with. There was no attempt to mix it up geographically.

The end result of this team-building exercise? Almost no one got to know anyone else other than on a very superficial level. Oh, and a team picture was taken. Within a month half of the people in the picture—including, sadly, the author—had had a haircut.

The moral of this story is not that anyone was particularly malevolent. Their intentions were good. Our manager was a great guy, one of the best we had worked for. But the execution and timing could not have been worse. Consequently, the remaining team was more demoralized than ever. Or at the very least, no better off than when we started and at a not insignificant cost to the company.

This lack of team building happened because there was very little *real* interaction. In order for team members to get to know each other, they need to perform exercises where they work toward a common goal as in the aforementioned escape room.

So, what does this have to do with meetings? There are two connections.

1. Meetings are a way to help build a project team.
2. In the context of a meeting, there is some *instant team building* needed.

Keep these two connections in mind as you read the stories and read about the models, tools, and techniques.

To Build a Project Team, You Need Trust and Psychological Safety

As trust and psychological safety are so fundamental to team building, perhaps especially in projects, we start with this important section.

Building Trust

Let's start by understanding how important trust really is. According to an outstanding HBR article, Begin with Trust, by Frances X. Frei and Anne Morriss (https://hbr.org/2020/05/begin-with-trust),

> Trust is the reason we're willing to exchange our hard-earned paychecks for goods and services, pledge our lives to another person in marriage, cast a ballot for someone who will represent our interests. We rely on laws and contracts as safety nets, but even they are ultimately built on trust in the institutions that enforce them.

So sure, we think you can agree that trust is important—in life and in project teams. One of us was the project director for a high-stakes deployment of an Olympics telecom, video, and data network. The network project was a remarkable success and provided flawless Olympic coverage. The single most important factor in this success was trust. The project manager evoked trust in his experience, his transparent communication style, and despite (or perhaps because of) a military background, he was undyingly empathetic to his team members.

This aligns exactly with what experts say are the components of trust. According to Frei and Morriss, there are three elements to trust. If any of them wobble—meaning that they become unsteady or not achieved— trust cannot exist. The three elements are (from the perspective of your team members):

- **Authenticity**: When you (the leader) communicate with me, it's truly the real you and not an act.
- **Logic**: You have sound judgment and the capability to do the work.
- **Empathy**: You care about me and my success.

These all must be in place in your team, and as a servant leader, it's your job to be sure that you've established and maintained them throughout the project. There is a very powerful TED talk in which author Frances Frei reviews her experience with Uber in building trust. She reviews ways in which each of the elements in her *Trust Triangle* can be degraded or boosted. To summarize her advice:

For an empathy wobble (the most common wobble), the antidote is being there for your team members. Avoid the "uh-huh, uh-huh" while looking at your mobile device. That evokes the opposite of empathy.

If you have logic wobbles, it's either from truly not having the capability or reasoning to do the work, or more likely it has to do with the way you communicate and inspire the fact that indeed you do. Hone your skills of storytelling and presentation to fix those logic wobbles.

The most difficult to identify and fix is the authenticity wobble. The obvious solution is to really be yourself—which is easy when you're with others like yourself. It's more difficult in a diverse group. Frei says of this: "Pay less attention to what you think people want to hear from you and far more attention to what your authentic, awesome self needs to say."

www.ted.com/talks/frances_frei_how_to_build_and_rebuild_trust?language=en

---

War Story—Demonstrating Empathy With a Bit of Theatrical Flair

For a global pharmaceutical company project that would create significant change for employees, I partnered with the CEO to do a road show at all their global locations. We created a skit to engage employees in the change that was happening. Each townhall meeting started with the CEO presenting the *why* of the change from the perspective of the organization—all about the financials. Lots of spreadsheets and graphs!

After about 10 minutes, I pushed him (gently of course!) off the stage, pulled up a chair, shut down the slide deck, and the meeting transitioned to talking about change from the perspective of the employees—the *WIIFM*. We played this skit on an every other year basis for about three years. What a great way to start off a major project at the company!

—Gina Abudi, Change Management Expert

Encouraging Psychological Safety (Adapted With Permission, From Carol Osterweil's *Neuroscience for Project Success*)

Psychological safety is "The belief that the work environment is safe for interpersonal risk taking ... feeling able to speak up with relevant ideas questions or concerns. It is present when colleagues trust and respect each other and feel able—even obligated—to be candid."†

This definition, from Amy Edmondson's book, *The Fearless Organization*, Wiley, is deceptively simple, and the ramifications profound. Without psychological safety, there are some detrimental symptoms, such as when a team member keeps quiet even though they can see something wrong—technically, or ethically. You see it when a team member fails to suggest a really great new idea because they're afraid they'll be ridiculed. And you see it in ritualized board meetings and team meetings where groupthink prevails or the risk of being cast as the dissenting voice is just too high.

When psychological safety is low, we secretly fear being punished, humiliated, or ostracized for speaking the truth as we see it. Low psychological safety gets in the way of team performance and project delivery. And, when you can't deliver the outcomes you've promised, it gets in the way of personal success.

A great example is Google's Project Aristotle. Project Aristotle was a multiyear research program that set out to identify what makes Google's most effective project teams so effective. What they found was that who is on the team matters far less than how the team members interact, structure their work and view their contributions.

It comes down to the group's norms of behavior and five key dimensions:

- *Psychological safety*—is it safe to take risks and be vulnerable in front of each other?
- *Dependability*—can we count on each other to do high quality work on time?
- *Structure and clarity*—are our goals, roles, and execution plans clear?

---

† www.strategy-business.com/article/How-Fearless-Organizations-Succeed.

- *Meaning of the work*—are we working on something that is personally important?
- *Impact of work*—do we fundamentally believe that the work we are doing matters?

Project Aristotle demonstrated that of these five dimensions, psychological safety stands head and shoulders above the rest—indeed, it is a prerequisite for the other four.

Team Development and Performance Models

The Tuckman Model

Psychologist Bruce Tuckman (1965) published a famous study where he identified what's now known as Tuckman's stages of group development—four stages that teams go through that are inevitable for their growth (he later added a fifth stage). Those stages are (see Figure 6.4):

- Forming
- Storming
- Norming
- Performing
- Adjourning (or mourning)

Forming

In forming, the team meets and gets to know each other. Initially, team members are more focused on themselves and less on the team. The individuals look to the leader for direction and are still uncertain, not only of

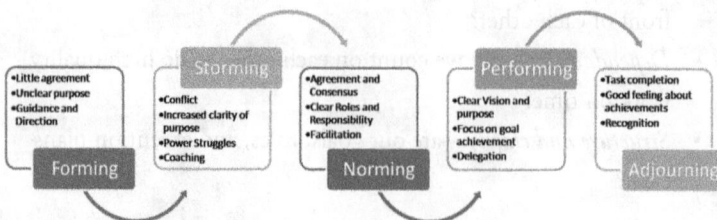

Figure 6.4 The five stages of team development
Source: Okpalad, based on Tuckman and Jensen (1977).

what the scope of their work is but also their role and responsibility in it. People are also uncertain about how to behave, what to say, even whether jokes are appropriate. Needless to say, they're not yet a team; at this point what you have is a gathering of individuals.

At this early stage, the team is looking for leadership. You must establish clear goals and objectives and be cognizant of the fact that you'll soon be entering storming. And be decisive—this is exactly what the team needs right now.

Storming

There's a good reason this stage is called storming. In this stage, individuals are still getting to know each other, but they've now formed opinions about what each brings to the project. This stage is where conflicts and personality clashes start to arise. Tuckman says that some teams never grow out of this stage. In that case, while they may fulfill the objectives of the project, it will be a more painful process than if they had resolved their conflicts. Remember also that the conflict could be with the *project*. In other words, a team member may not be fully on board with the overall project deliverable or one of its objectives. You'll need to have one-on-one conversations with such team members.

Tolerance and patience are important. The team leader is still very much in a directive status, not yet feeling comfortable delegating leadership. She may initially need more frequent meetings to find out how team members are working together and will likely be more heavily involved in conflict management. Storming can be destructive to the team and will lower motivation if it's allowed to get out of control—especially if the conflict becomes personal.

Timely Tangent: A Musical Example of Conflict (*Storming*) Yielding Benefits

Conflict in teams, and in meetings, is not necessarily bad. It's definitely a bad thing if it is personalized. However, in situations where high-level performance, creativity, and ingenuity are required, conflict should be expected and is—counterintuitively—a contributor to success. Witness this video (https://vimeo.com/139848837) in which four musicians start by introducing their own instrument, and themselves, with a "look at me, aren't I wonderful?" attitude. As each musician gets their opening solo, they are in a highly competitive mode. They see each other as competitors (for attention) and not collaborators. You will see alliances form and break; you will see what appears to be nastiness. The conflict manifests itself in each of the performers trying to out-do each other with all sorts of crazy new ways to show off their talents, involving some pretty crazy innovations. In fact, as they try to out-do each other, they, slowly but very surely, realize that … wait a second … we are all good, and we will be even better together. They acknowledge their mutual excellence, and start to get energy from the crowd, and end with near-perfect choreography like a well-oiled machine that has been together forever.

The thing is: without the conflict, the competitiveness, showing off, the new ideas and techniques would not have arisen at all. On the other hand, if it had escalated or had been personalized, it could have been highly destructive. This team managed to self-regulate that level of conflict. In some cases, however, a servant leader would be required.

In fact, in this video, the entire performance—including the competitiveness and conflict—is scripted and well-rehearsed, but the point is well made.

Disagreements within the team can make members stronger, more versatile, and able to work more effectively as a team. Further, it's during the storming stage that you'll likely find the team's more innovative ideas popping up, because competition and good arguments can stimulate creativity.

Some teams will never exit storming. If a team never gets past this stage, it will be more difficult for it to deliver on time if at all. The most important things at this point are to build trust as well as resolve conflict. Team building can help to establish trust. As to conflict management, it's wisest to initially allow team members to work out their own conflicts. Step in to resolve them only if they can't.

Although a detailed treatment of conflict management is beyond the scope of this book, we have found that the Thomas–Kilmann conflict mode instrument (TKI, Kilmann 2018, Figure 6.5) has significant value. This model yields five modes of dealing with conflict. The five modes are:

- Competing
- Avoiding
- Accommodating
- Collaborating
- Compromising

According to TKI, each person has a default mode where they generally operate. But project managers need to be able to move easily between those modes for differing project situations.

One of the authors recently took an online TKI exam and found that his predominant style was accommodating with a strong second of compromising. He was happy to note this as he also functions as a coach. He also notes that he was low on competing (yay!) but needs to bring his collaborating up a bit.

That said, let's get back to team building.

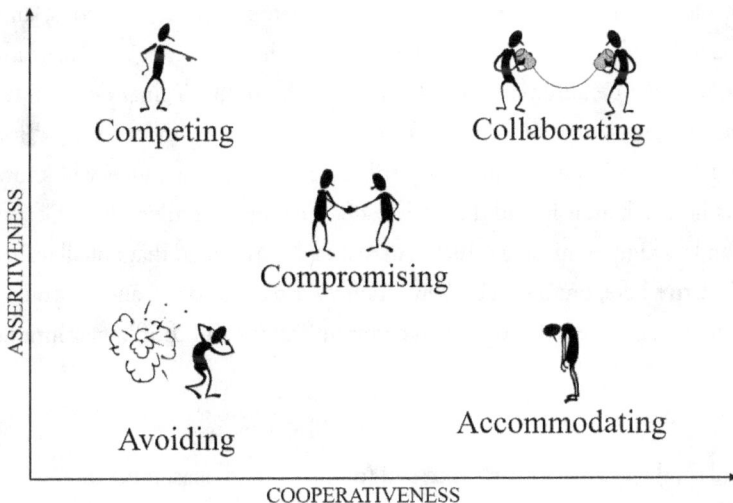

Figure 6.5 Mapping the five modes of dealing with conflict based on assertiveness versus cooperativeness

Norming

In this stage, the team starts to *cohere* as a team. If any members can't get along, they have by now left—or *should* have left—the team. The others are starting to work as a unit toward the project's objectives. The team members—and it's now a team rather than a group of individuals—are not only sharing responsibility but are acting more cooperatively with each other. It's in this stage where team members learn to trust one another. And while one person is still very much a team lead, she's now able to allow the team to make its own decisions. If the leader is lost, or if there's any other disruption, it's possible for the team to fall back to a previous stage.

You must be careful not to slip back to an earlier stage for other reasons, such as unresolved conflict, hurt feelings, or lack of trust. If you need to do more team building, do so. If a person needs to be removed from the team, then that's what must be done. But be sure to do it in way that is respectful. (Note that if a new team member joins, you will likely slip back to an earlier stage, much in the way that a new person joining a social situation changes the dynamic.)

Performing

In reality, this means *high-performing* teams. By this time, team members are motivated and knowledgeable. They're competent, autonomous, and able to handle the decision-making process without supervision. The team should now be automatically locked-in to the project's final deliverables and outcomes, and without any direction, are keeping them in mind for all project decisions. Conflict may still arise, but team members will know best how to handle it, and the team leader is happy to let them do it. Group morale is high in this stage. Tuckman makes the argument that not all teams will arrive here, but it's incumbent upon your team to do so and for you to help them get there through open communications and conflict resolution.

Adjourning

And so, the team has been successful (or not...) and, alas, must disengage. This stage is sometimes called mourning—you've spent so much time building up a team relationship, and now you have to, in a sense, tear it down. Some team members may become emotional and want to stay together. You hear of this often in situations such as movie sets, where actors and crew are together for an intense month or two and develop a sense of family. For example, the entire cast of *A Fish Called Wanda* stayed together for a totally different film called *Fierce Creatures*.

As we mentioned, a key component of having an effective team is trust. Team members must trust that they can rely on each other to get the job done well. They must feel comfortable that team members will take individual responsibility and be accountable for their actions.

According to *A Guide to the Project Management Body of Knowledge, PMBOK® Guide Sixth Edition*, high team performance can be achieved by employing these behaviors:

- Using open and effective communication
- Creating team-building opportunities
- Developing trust among team members
- Managing conflicts in a constructive manner
- Encouraging collaborative problem-solving
- Encouraging collaborative decision making

Advantages and Challenges of Diversity in (Project) Teams

NOTE: Adapted from Indeed.com from August 2021. Also enhanced by an in-class exercise that one of the authors uses in a *Project Communications and Leadership* course created by that author.

Following are some of the many advantages of diversity in a project team. Although this could apply to any team, it's even more important in a project, where the team is assembled from different organizations and is—by design—temporary.

Advantages

- Increased creativity and innovation
  - A wide variety of backgrounds fuels creative thinking.
- Enhanced problem-solving and decision making
  - You have an expanded set of experience—people who have seen this very problem—or one like it—before.

- Strengthened skillsets
  - The team becomes a learning organization if led properly.
- Possibility of quickened response time for customers
  - You have the expertise on the team, you don't have to go to a specialist organization.
- Heightened employee engagement
  - A sense of "no matter who I am, I belong" becomes inherent in the team.
- Improved company reputation
  - Diversity, equity, and inclusion (DE&I) is becoming an increasingly important way in which people view your organization.
  - Also, potential employees often shop for organizations for whom this is an important critical success factor (CSF).
- Strengthened team morale
  - Like a sports team with different contributors (think rugby: left wing, blind-side blanker, loose-head prop), if trust exists combined with diversity, team confidence goes up and morale gets a boost.

Disadvantages (Challenges) of a Diverse Team

Some of these disadvantages are simply the flip side of the advantages, for example, the wide variety of backgrounds could easily lead to language, culture, and bias issues.

However, for completeness, here is a list of the challenges:

- Communication barriers
  - Native language, colloquial expressions, accents, grammar, body language differences, even sets of acronyms that a technical team member may use and considers common use but are cryptic and off-putting hieroglyphs to those unfamiliar with the technology—any of these can be challenges.
- Culture differences
  - There is of course a negative risk (a threat) that the team's cultural differences create conflict. This can affect the per-

formance, creativity, and workflow of the team, which may impact workplace relationships. This is where the skills of a project leader really come in to play. You are the one to create an environment of trust and inclusion.

- Slower decision making
  - o We know that we said earlier that diversity can expedite decision making. But the reverse is also true, especially if you need to consider a huge number of proposed solutions.
- Biases and heuristics
  - o Let's take that example of a technical team reviewing a marketing solution for your project. There is risk (a threat) that the technical team will automatically discount (perhaps even berate) the marketing solution as smoke and mirrors, or that the marketing team may automatically discount (and even berate) the technical solution as needlessly detailed and too slow.
  - o The same sort of threat may occur with biases regarding national culture. Watch this carefully; again, as a project leader, your goal is to get as much out of your team as possible without these biases.

Gersick's Model of Punctuated Equilibrium

Equally important and impactful to understanding how and why great teams form and perform (yet is often lesser known in the workplace) is the research of Yale professor Connie Gersick. Dr. Gersick developed and introduced a group development model known as *Punctuated Equilibrium*, a conceptual perspective by paleo-biologist Niles Eldredge and Stephen Gould (1972) that explained how species adapt and new species emerge and adapted the concept to explain how project groups progressed and accomplished their work.

We include this model because we have seen this behavior in teams (and we are willing to bet you have as well). If you've ever seen a team *wake up* about halfway through a project, suddenly realizing that they now have only two weeks left on a four-week project and have to scurry, you have seen punctuated equilibrium.

Through Gersick's model, we can begin to appreciate the dynamics (how project teams move through team development) and the dramatics (how project teams function as they move through team development) observable in the team-building processes. Specifically, punctuated equilibrium allows us to understand teams and what to expect as they engage on their assigned work and where opportunities to maximize their performance might exist.

Gersick reminds us that team formation and performance is not static nor a linear process, it's fluid and yet somewhat predictable. Dr. Gersick's research sheds light on how teams move through their development inside the workplace. Team development is not as rigid as the construction of a house—the foundation and structure only offer opportunities for incremental adaptations—rather teams can completely reconfigure themselves and their approaches during a project at certain times. This is an important insight to have when thinking about project teams in the contemporary day (more so post-COVID-19) who face a constant fog of volatile, uncertain, complex, and ambiguous (VUCA) factors in the performance of their duties.

Teams develop as the complex adaptive systems they are—which makes sense—humans are complex beings. It follows that groups of humans would tend to add a whole new layer of complexity. Punctuated equilibrium helps us account for this actuality by allowing space for the presence of diverse approaches and configurations to be used by project teams. The model also provides predictability on what we as project leaders can expect as teams approach and accomplish their assigned work. We note here that adaptive and Agile are synonymous for our purposes—and you can see that the idea of teams developing adaptively fits well with an Agile mindset.

Let's go back to an earlier analogy and imagine a project team as a sports team. The punctuated equilibrium model establishes the idea that team plays develop distinctively different during phases of the game work assignment/time left until delivery. Dr. Gersick's research observed that project groups distinctively localize their approach to a work assignment—just like a team approaches how they initially prepare and play the game.

Then about halfway through the allotted time for work to be completed (the midpoint), each project group researched (varying in different work contexts) exhibited a dramatic change and reconfigured how they played the rest of the game (See Figure 6.6). This can be thought of in the same sense as a university or professional basketball team that often makes significant adjustments during the halftime of the game. Notably, Gersick (1998) elevated the importance for project leaders to pay attention in this transition period, given the critical opportunities it provides due to three key conditions occurring in it.

- Members are experienced enough with the work to understand the meaning of contextual requirements.
- Resources have used up enough of their time that they feel they must get on with the task.
- Resources still have enough time left that they can make significant changes in the design of their products.

Some of the changes that Dr. Gersick's research discovered were:

- Adjustments in engaging with different stakeholders external to the project
- Adopting different perspectives on how to approach the work
- Changing overall work patterns used to accomplish the work.

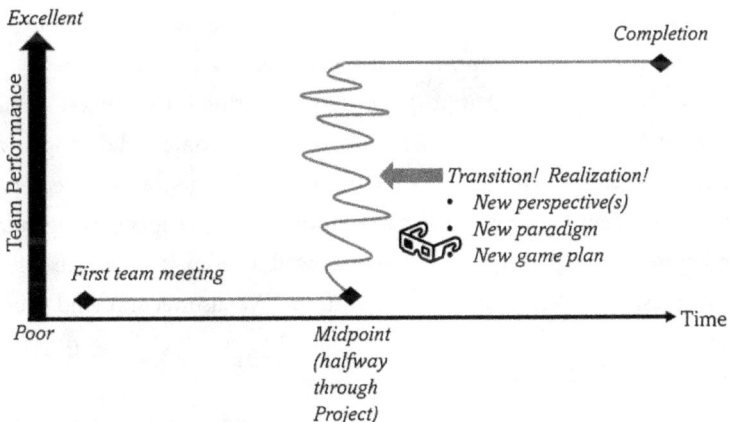

Figure 6.6 *Gersick's punctuated equilibrium model—that aha moment*

This transition (midpoint) period reconfigures the approach that brings the project team to work completion.

When we as project leaders understand the punctuated equilibrium model, we can better *tune in* and optimize support for our teams in concert with the shifting states of stability and disruption they will necessarily progress through during different phases of the game (work assignment). Dr. Gersick's research offers us an important consideration to practices leading the management of project teams. The development of project teams is something that discontinuous but is also navigable. The punctuated equilibrium model offers us as project leaders a guide to navigate our understanding and effort to best engage and help steer the project team's development to successful outcomes sought by us, the project team, and the impacted stakeholders associated to the work the project team is working to accomplish.

Some Tools for Team Building in Hybrid Teams

One of our colleagues, Bentzy Goldman, founder of the startup Perflo created a tool of the same name for teams that can be used to self-assess their effectiveness on a continuous basis and provide team-based micro-assessments and team analytics on various metrics that contribute to a team's wellbeing and performance.

One of the important themes measured in Perflo is meeting effectiveness. This software solicits feedback from team members (and leaders) directly in Slack and Microsoft Teams and provides results to the team with opportunities for improvement suggestions.

We have identified that how you start a meeting is the biggest influencer of how that meeting will be run and how people feel during and after that meeting. Things that are crucial are starting off light, checking in with the team on a nonwork-related level, setting a super clear agenda and time to be spent on each topic, as well as who is responsible for any notes, follow-up e-mail or action items. We also recommend these tools:

- **Butter**: video conferencing with timed agendas, www.butter.us/
- **Twist**: asynchronous messaging app, https://twist.com/

- **Spike:** collaborative email platform, www.spikenow.com/
- **Slido:** participant engagement built into Zoom, Webex, and so on, www.slido.com

Summary

Project work gets done via teams, and it is the main work of the project leader to build a cohesive, responsible, contributory environment for that team to develop. Teams go through stages in developing, and it is incumbent on the project leader to understand those stages, including those times (which will occur!) in which conflict arises. Using the tips and tools, methods, and models from this chapter will help you build the high performing team you need to make your project successful.

References

Damn Yankees clip: https://youtu.be/Ry8CpIg2fvU.

Edmondson, A. 2018. *The Fearless Organization: Creating Psychological Safety in the Workplace for Learning, Innovation and Growth.* Wiley.

Eldredge, N. and S.J. Gould. 1972. "Punctuated Equilibria: An Alternative to Phyletic Gradualism." In *Models in Paleobiology,* T.J.M. Schopf, pp. 82–115. San Francisco: Freeman Cooper & Co.

Gersick, C.J.G. 1988. "Time and Transition in Work Teams: Toward a New Model of Group Development." *Academy of Management Journal* 31, no. 1, pp. 9–41.

https://hbr.org/2017/01/great-teams-are-about-personalities-not-just-skills.

Kilmann, R.H. 2018. https://kilmanndiagnostics.com/brief-overview-of-the-tki-assessment/.

Osterweil, C. 2022. *Neuroscience for Project Success: Why People Behave as They Do.* Association for Project Management (APM).

Tuckman, B. 1965. Developmental sequence in small groups. *Psychological Bulletin, 63*(6), pp. 384–399.

Tuckman and Jensen. 1997. https://culture724592608.wordpress.com/category/contemporary-leadership-styles/.

CHAPTER 7

Deviled Eggs

Turn Your Project Team Into an Idea Incubator

Coauthored by Karin Hurt and David Dye (With Some Paprika From Your Authors)

Key Takeaways

- Speaking up during a meeting may be challenging for a variety of reasons.
- Team members may lack confidence or feel their ideas are not welcomed.
- Techniques such as fear foraging may help teams to share and discuss what's in their hearts and minds with candor.
- Speaking up freely can prevent not only relatively minor project issues but may also prevent larger catastrophic ones.

Karin Hurt and David Dye are the CEOs of *Let's Grow Leaders, and International Leadership Development Company.* Their latest book is *Courageous Cultures: How to Build Teams of Micro-Innovators, Problem Solvers and Customer Advocates* (Harper Collins).

Has this ever happened to you? You run into a major issue with your project, and a team member confides, "I've been worried about that for months, but I didn't think it was my place to bring it up, especially at your meeting."

Or in a lessons learned session, one of your PMs shares her idea for next time. The idea is fantastic, and it would have saved you weeks of frustration—*this* time. When you ask why she didn't share her idea earlier, she shrugs and say, "Well, you didn't ask until now."

You want your team to speak up, share their ideas, and raise their hands when they have a concern—in general, and at your project meetings. But many project managers focus more on the devil in the details, than on playing devil's advocate.

It can feel safer to follow the plan than to question it. But in turbulent, uncertain times, you don't just need your project managers doing, you need them consistently asking, "How can we do this better?" or "What might go wrong?"

Why Speaking Up Can Be Hard

In our research conducted with the University of North Colorado Social Research Lab, employees told us why they hold back ideas.

- They don't think leadership wants their ideas (67 percent say their manager acts according to the notion "This is the way we've always done it").
- No one asks (49 percent said they're not regularly asked for their ideas).
- They lack the confidence to share their ideas (we call this FOSU—fear of speaking up, and 40 percent have it).
- They lack the skills to share their ideas (45 percent say there's no training available for problem-solving and critical thinking).
- They think nothing will ever happen, so why bother (50 percent said they believed if they shared an idea, it wouldn't be taken seriously).

And the ideas they keep to themselves were not trivial, like "let's have kombucha in the break room or start a series of virtual taco Tuesdays." They were ideas to improve the customer experience, the employee experience, or productivity in a process.

Here's the good news. There are practical and easy-to-implement ways you can invite your team to contribute micro-innovations and ideas to improve your organization.

We call this cultivating curiosity, and it's part of a seven-step process for building more innovative and courageous teams that we share in *Courageous Cultures: How to Build Teams of Micro-Innovators, Problem Solvers and Customer Advocates.*

Practical Techniques to Help Your Team Speak Up and Share Ideas

The Fear Forage

One of our favorite techniques for cultivating curiosity is a fear forage. At a kickoff or early project team meeting, give your team an index card and invite each team member to put an *H* on the front of the card and write their hopes for the project, and on the back, have them write an *F* and write their fears. Collect the cards and read out the themes. (In a virtual environment, use Google Forms or other survey software.)

The fear forage is an easy way for people to share and discuss what's in their hearts and minds with candor ideas they may have not expressed if you had just asked the question aloud.

We recently used this technique with a very senior project team comprised of executives from across the company's five brands. They had all written the same fears: "I do not trust my peers will go back and execute this plan."

Can you imagine the wasted time if had not addressed those fears? Together, they built an accountability plan so that everyone had confidence they weren't alone, and the project moved forward.

Courageous Questions

Another simple technique is mastering the art of courageous questions. A courageous question differs from a generic "How can we be better?" question in three ways. It's specific, meaning you ask about one idea. It's vulnerable; it assumes that improvement is possible. Finally, you ask from genuine curiosity—not to immediately respond.

For example, you could ask one or more of the following at a brainstorming meeting:

- What's one policy that really annoys our customers?
- What is the biggest roadblock to your productivity right now?
- If we could do one thing to help this project succeed, what would that be?
- What's one way we could improve the efficiency of this process?

Owning the U.G.L.Y.

If you have a specific strategic initiative or issue where you need great ideas, you can pair four of our favorite courageous questions together into an *Own the U.G.L.Y.* brainstorming session.

Begin with clarity by identifying the topic for discussion.

With regard to _____ (fill in your strategic initiative here).

Then move to curiosity by asking attendees four courageous questions related to this topic:

- **U**: What are we underestimating (e.g., competitive pressures, technology needs)?
- **G**: What's got to go? (What must we stop doing to be successful?)
- **L**: Where are we losing? (who is doing this better?)
- **Y**: Where are we missing the Yes (new markets, totally new approaches)?

Working through each of the questions together at the meeting helps the team rapidly surface challenges and opportunities. Our clients have used this method for a wide range of issues, such as getting input into their diversity, equity, and inclusion (DE&I) strategy, launching a new product, and building out their remote work approach.

Help Your Team Bring You Better Ideas

In addition to asking courageous questions, another way to help your team feel confident in sharing their ideas is to give them criteria to follow, to prequalify their idea for presenting it at a meeting.

Teach them the I.D.E.A. model to position their ideas.

I—Interesting

Why is this idea interesting? What strategic problem does it solve? How will results improve from this idea (e.g., customer experience, employee retention, efficiency)?

D—Doable

Is this idea something we could actually do? How would we make it happen? What would make it easier or more difficult?

E—Engaging

Who would we need to engage to make this happen? Why should they support it? Where are we most likely to meet resistance?

A—Actions

What are the most important actions needed to try this? How would we start? You may notice a connection between this IDEA technique and the SMART technique for metrics (specific, measurable, achievable, relevant, and time-bound). That's not a coincidence. You will want to measure the applicability of the idea.

How You Respond at the Meeting Makes All the Difference

Recall the research findings: 50 percent of respondents said they believed that if they share an idea, it won't be taken seriously. Even more concerning is that the number one reason people said they would keep a micro-innovation to themselves (56 percent) is concern that they wouldn't get credit for their idea. And then there are the 67 percent who said their leadership operates from "this is how we've always done it."

Feeling Ignored. Not Getting Credit. Believing Nothing Will Happen

What do these findings have in common? These aren't failures to ask—these are failures to respond and respond well. Indeed, they are failures of leadership to establish the psychological safety needed to bring up wacky new ideas and to question something that is just plain wrong. How you respond to the ideas of your project team will either build momentum or crush innovation.

The Solution Is to Respond With Regard

Responding with regard means you receive ideas in ways that value the other person, build momentum, improve your project team's strategic thinking, and generate more useful ideas.

There are three steps to respond with regard. First, thank them for their idea. Then add information about next steps, other priorities, or critical data. Finally, conclude with an invitation to continue thinking and contributing.

For example, if team member Kim suggests an idea to eliminate a meeting that you know your remote team members value, you might respond with regard by saying:

> *Kim, thank you for thinking about how we can be more efficient with our meetings—I appreciate you looking for ways we can do this. With regard to the meeting you mentioned, I do know that several of our international team members have mentioned that this is the way they feel connected to the rest of us, and it's been useful for resolving some of the roadblocks we've encountered with this project. I'd love to get your thoughts on how we can improve our meeting efficiency and maintain the connection and problem-solving opportunities with our global team.*

If you want more courage, innovation, and problem-solving on your project team, you don't have to start with big challenging problems. Begin with small problems that frustrate your project team. Be clear that your meetings are safe places where questions and ideas matter, and that the project leadership really does appreciate ideas and input with impunity. And then, get curious and involve your team in the process of making their lives better.

So, by now, you are asking yourself—why do we call this chapter *Deviled Eggs*?

Well, it starts with the concept of an *egg*, the beginning of an idea that may bring your organization much success or prevent a significant project disaster (or a disaster that takes place after your project is turned over to operations). To hatch and become more than an oblong spheroid (that's one for you geometry freaks), eggs need care. They need incubation, receptivity, and warmth. You've seen that in the section from Karin Hurt and David Dye, with their concept of responding with regard. So, what the devil is the deviled part?

That comes from the concept of *devil's advocacy*. This ties in very closely with psychological safety, a concept we discussed in Chapter 6. The origin of the phrase devil's advocacy is fascinating. From www .phrases.org.uk:

> *There are various mentions in Vatican records dating from the early 1500s of an informal role called "Diaboli Advocatus." In 1587, the administration of Pope Sixtus V established the formal post of Promoter of the Faith, known colloquially as the "Advocatus Diaboli." The job description wasn't especially onerous, until someone was nominated for either beatification and canonization, at which point the "Devil's Advocate" was expected to draw up a list of arguments against the nominee becoming blessed or canonized.*

This was a person (an actual formal position in the Church!) whose job it was—acting not as themselves, but as an advocate for the other side of the story—to speak truth to power. Nowadays, this is a role that one takes on, perhaps at a meeting, in which they feel free to take a contrary view, to poke holes in the logic the team is proposing, to catch problems early on.

Those in the field of IT will recognize this as the white hat hackers, who are brought in to intentionally find security gaps in a system. In a way, they are playing the devil's advocate role.

How does this tie back to meetings? To answer that, simply look at projects and products with disastrous results. For example, take the BP Macondo Well project, known more popularly as the Deepwater

Horizon incident. You can watch the first 25 minutes of the film *Deepwater Horizon* and see the interchanges in meetings where BP (with John Malkovich playing BP executive Donald Vidrine and Kurt Russel playing Jimmy Harrell of Transocean), Russell (as Jimmy Harrell) is unsuccessful but does a great job illustrating devil's advocacy and speaking truth to power.

As mentioned previously, there are other very visible, very real, very sad examples of avertable disasters if there was more psychological safety in meetings (see references for details):

- The infamous O-Rings in the Space Shuttle Challenger
- Volkswagen's *Dieselgate* scandal
- The natural gas explosions during a Columbia Gas of Massachusetts repair project
- The crashes and grounding of the 737 Max 8—see the Netflix documentary *Downfall* and U.S. National Transportation Safety Board in our references

The key for project leaders and facilitators of project meetings is to create an environment where it is okay and safe to bring up a contrary point of view, and as Hurt and Dye say, respond with regard.

For much more on the gas explosions and the Boeing 737 Max 8 incidents, see the chapter *Irresponsible Project Management* by coauthor Rich Maltzman in the DeGruyter publication, The Handbook of Responsible Project Management, published in 2022.

There are two parts to this, of course—there is (1) the environment, for which you, as a project leader, are responsible, and (2) there is the complementary willingness of the participants to speak up. For the former, the work of Karin Hurt and David Dye, contributors to this chapter, as well as Harvard Business School professor Amy Edmondson, is quite valuable.

For the latter, there is excellent coverage of this in Jim Detert's book, *Choosing Courage*, and his website, http://jimdetert.com. The BEP book *Public Relations Ethics: Senior PR Pros Tell Us How to Speak Up and Keep Your Job* also has this as a main topic.

Summary

The very nature of a meeting, which is intended to discuss issues and foster collaboration, may conversely be detrimental to the free sharing of ideas and risks that are necessary to discuss. In order to overcome this for the betterment of the project, it is wise to solicit all ideas and make the meeting a safe space, provide psychological safety, for those ideas that may run counter to the group.

References

Boeing 737 Max 8 – US National Transportation Safety Board report: www.ntsb .gov/investigations/accidentreports/reports/asr1901.pdf.
Columbia Gas of Massachusetts Merrimack Valley explosions: www.wgbh.org/ news/term/fire-in-the-valley-the-podcast.
O-Rings/Challenger: https://neuroleadership.com/your-brain-at-work/challenger-disaster-speaking-up/.
Volkswagen 'Dieselgate' scandal: https://arielle.com.au/top-harvard-professors-weigh-in-on-vw-dieselgate-what-it-means-for-leadership-culture-and-the-future-of-work/.

CHAPTER 8

Working in a Multicultural Environment

Key Takeaways

- Culture is an important part of any project environment and must be taken into consideration.
- Both organizational and national culture have impacts on the project.
- Spend some time studying the culture you're entering in order not only to communicate better but also to avoid any faux pas.
- When in Rome, do as the Romans do.

Just to shake things up a little bit, let's kick this chapter off with a war story from one of our authors:

War Story—Thanks, Mr. Big Shot!

I was asked to teach a PMP certification class for a quasi-governmental organization in Brussels. I rented a car for the three-day training and arrived at the facility at the same time as the small (six guys) group. I should have known from the start that things weren't going to go well. I had a bunch of training materials (books, flip charts, etc.), and while I was getting them out of the car—and could have used some help—they all walked away and went into the building.

That was probably the best part of class as it was all downhill from there. It started okay when I was beginning to teach, but during the course of the three days, the in-charge guy continually kept challenging things that I said and trying to tell his team (they all worked for him) alternative versions of what I was saying. The problem is that I was not there to give my personal opinion but to convey information that they needed to pass the exam. At one point late in the week, he actually came up to the board and tried to show his team what earned value was and how it was calculated. All of which would have been fine if (1) I invited him and (2) I didn't for some reason know how to teach it.

At the end of the class, I asked for a lessons learned about what had transpired in the class. They told me it would have gone better if I'd sent them copies of the Project Management Body of Knowledge in advance. Then they all would have read it and then asked me questions. I told them that that was not my teaching style, and that it would not work for a certification exam. Further, if I'd known that, I never would have gone over. I lost this one sitting in the airport in New York.

The real problem is that the guy in charge could not stand someone else in the room being smarter than him or knowing more so he felt it necessary to undermine my authority. The icing on the cake was when I happened to mention that the one thing in the book I'd never done before was use critical chain. He said that that invalidated the entire training. Which is ridiculous because no instructor I know has done everything in the book, much less use the fairly esoteric critical chain (since dropped from PMBOK® Guide.)

Last note—the one thing I'm indebted to Mr. Big Shot for is a side conversation explaining how the Walloons and the Flemish do not get along and have separate cultures. I would say all things being considered; the Walloons are well off not knowing this guy.

—Author Jim Stewart

We'll certainly talk about meetings in this chapter. But our focus is primarily on culture. And we're not just talking the cultures of, say, England compared with Chile, but also organizational culture and cultures *within* a country. This chapter also includes cultures of functional groups like sales teams or software developers or architects. Understanding and acclimating to culture other than your own—inside or outside of meetings—will greatly increase your chance of project success.

Considering that projects are a means to implement strategy, it is interesting to note that, according to management guru Peter Drucker: Culture eats strategy for breakfast.

So, unless we want to *be breakfast*, we had better increase our expertise in the area of culture.

Let's start with a definition of culture from an expert we trust—Geert Hofstede. Hofstede, dubbed a guru and "the man who put corporate culture—literally—on the map," by *The Economist*, taught at the well-respected business school, the *Institut Européen d'Administration des Affaires* (INSEAD), near Paris, and in Hong Kong. He also taught for long spells in his home country of the Netherlands, at Maastricht University and the University of Tilburg.

Early in his career, Hofstede worked for IBM, where he conducted the research on which his career and reputation subsequently rested. What has become known as the Hofstede cultural orientation model is based on his study between 1967 and 1973 of IBM employees in 40 different countries. Although he passed away in 2020, his consultancy, under the leadership of his son, Gert Jan, continues to pursue and publish up-to-date corporate culture studies, including one on organizational culture called *Culture and Organizations—Software of the Mind*, and he's often cited as the central reference for all things related to cultural differences (see geerthofstede.com).

According to Hofstede Insights (2018):

> Culture is defined as the *collective mental programming* of the human mind which distinguishes one group of people from another. This programming influences patterns of thinking which are reflected in the meaning people attach to various aspects of life and which become crystallized in the institutions of a society.

Next, it's important for us to gain an appreciation of two distinct aspects of culture, organizational and national (country) culture. Next, we draw from Hofstede's research (Figure 8.1) by picking and choosing some of the dimensions from both organizational and national culture.

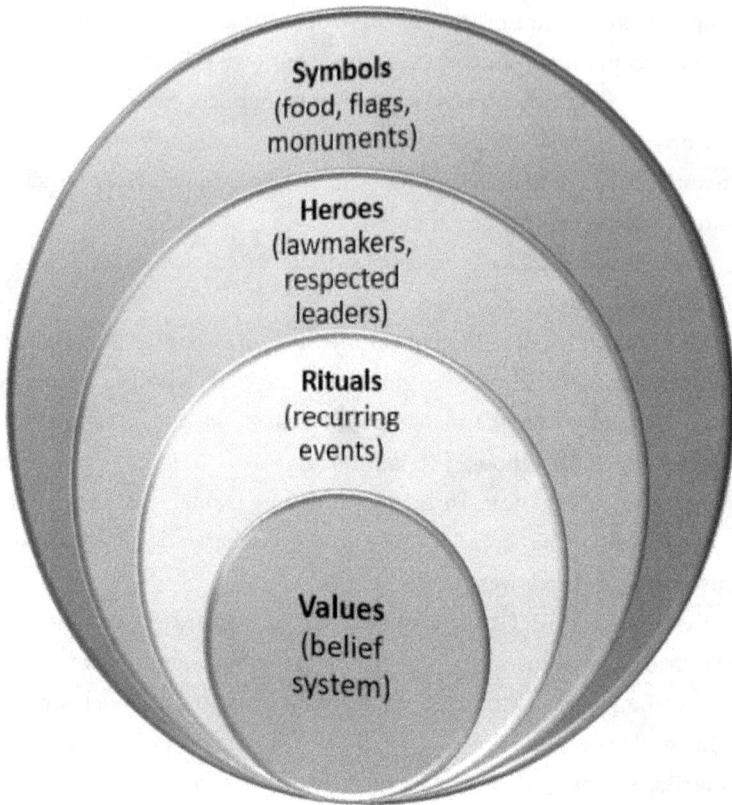

Figure 8.1 Culture—from values to symbols
Adapted from Hofstede (htttp://Hofstede-insights.com)

Organizational Culture

Organizational culture is defined as "the way in which members of an organization relate to each other, their work, and the outside world in comparison to other organizations. It can either enable or hinder an organization's strategy" (Hofstede Insights 2018). Hofstede and his son describe this in their book, *Cultures and Organizations: Software of the Mind.*

We have selected the dimensions of culture that most impact the success of your project planning meetings and apply those dimensions to your meetings.

Means-Oriented Versus Goal-Oriented

This dimension is closely connected to the effectiveness of the organization.

- In a means-oriented organizational culture, it's all about the *how*. People are process-oriented and less concerned with what, or how much gets done, and much more focused on the process. A classic example may be a customer service person at the Department of Motor Vehicles who is less interested in you getting your new license plates and more interested in making sure the forms are all completed exactly as they are supposed to be. ("Please fill these out in triplicate and then go to Window 3.")
- In a goal-oriented organizational culture, employees are primarily out to achieve specific goals or results, however they are achieved—they are all about the *what*. An example may be a start-up brewery, which really wants to get its first beers started and neglects to consider some of the regulatory processes they need to follow. One need only to look as far as Uber for an example in which the culture was one that focused only on the end result and seemed to completely ignore the means to get there. See our references for more details.

For project meetings, this aspect of organizational culture will be significant. In means-oriented cultures, you're likely to have strong buy-in for meetings—they recognize the fact that meetings are a means to an end. However, in goal-oriented cultures, you'll likely have trouble even getting people *to* meetings, and, if you are lucky enough to do so, you'll probably struggle to keep their attention.

Easygoing Work Discipline Versus Strict Work Discipline

- An easygoing work discipline culture is comfortable with lots of improvisation and surprises.
- A strict work discipline culture is the opposite—people are no-nonsense, punctual, and serious.

The connection is straightforward. In an easygoing culture, it's going to be difficult to get people to meetings on time—or perhaps even to get them to take assigned action items seriously. The opposite is true of a strict work discipline culture. However, it's not that black and white. People from an easygoing work discipline, when they finally show up, will likely do well in an open brainstorming session, while their strict work discipline cousins pine for a more structured activity.

As a project manager, you should be aware of this dimension of organizational culture. You may need to modify your style from time to time to accommodate both. For example: in a work breakdown structure (WBS) session—a concept we explore in Chapter 11—start on time and explain to people how you expect this strict discipline style to work. But be sure that when you develop the WBS, you allow and encourage creative, off-the-wall suggestions for content. Indicate that the end-time of the meeting is uncertain because you want to allow it to fully play out.

Local Versus Professional Organizations

This dimension is about how employees identify themselves. In a so-called local organization, employees tend to identify with the boss and/or the unit in which they work. "I'm in the XYZ Product Development Group," they're likely to say.

Conversely, in a professional organization, an employee instead identifies with their profession. "I'm a senior programmer," they're likely to say. As a project meeting facilitator, this will be important because part of your job is to be sure your project team really clicks as a team, which means that you need to watch out not only for cliques—small groups that may suboptimize the work you need to get done as one larger project team—but how they tend to form.

Open System Culture Versus Closed System Culture

- In an open system culture, newcomers are readily welcomed, and the working belief is that almost anyone could join the organization. Google touts its open culture.

- In a closed system organization, the belief is that one has to be special, or be initiated, to join the organization. This is typical of very focused technical organizations, especially those with treasured reputation, for example, Bell Laboratories.

Clearly, if you need to bring people together for project team meetings, you'll have much more trouble getting people past the storming stage (Chapter 6) in a closed system.

National Culture

National culture, like organizational culture, is made up of dimensions—this time cultural dimensions, which "represent independent preferences for one state of affairs over another that distinguish countries (rather than individuals) from each other" (Hofstede Insights 2018).

Here we present the cultural dimensions of national culture that most greatly affect project meetings. Again, we tie these dimensions directly to their effect on your meetings—how they may help or hinder them.

Power Distance Index (PDI)

- When the power distance index (PDI) is high, employees expect that everybody has their place (their rank), and higher rank automatically demands respect and has authority. Lower rank—well, they don't demand *anything*. They do what the higher-ranked person tells them to do.
- In societies with low PDI, people believe that power and authority should be equally distributed. As the leader of the meeting, you may see a high PDI as an advantage ("All hail the Project Manager, Great Leader Of This Meeting!"), but it can be a detriment. With high PDI (Malaysia, Guatemala, Panama, Philippines, Mexico, Venezuela, and China), those who perceive their power to be low won't interrupt or contribute, even when what they have to say may be critical.

As the facilitator, you need to be aware of this dimension and the fact that it may prevail in certain national cultures—and knowing this, poll the audience and invite participation frequently. In low PDI cultures (Austria, Israel, and Denmark), you won't have this problem, but you may have the other extreme—interruptions and disregard for authority. You may have to remind this audience that *you* own the meeting and assert control.

Individualism Versus Collectivism (IDV)

- Individualism (high IDV) means that employees prefer a loosely knit social framework in which individuals are expected to take care of and distinguish themselves.
- Collectivism (low IDV) is a preference for a group in which individuals can expect a family, village, or in this case, an organization to care for them in exchange for unquestioning loyalty.

For countries with high IDV (the United States, Australia, the United Kingdom, and the Netherlands), people will likely be a little less shy and more willing to be creative and/or take a stance on an issue. In the extreme, they may even showboat (a goblin!) and be less likely to be team players.

On the other hand, you may have to tease out contributions from low IDV countries such as many Central American countries, Pakistan, Japan, and Indonesia.

These same countries, however, are also more focused on team formation and team goals, but it's a mixed blessing: the team may form more quickly but may be less innovative and more risk-averse. This is a good segue to the next dimension—uncertainty avoidance.

Uncertainty Avoidance Index (UAI)

The uncertainty avoidance index (UAI) defines how a group feels with respect to uncertainty and ambiguity.

Think of a high UAI as being very risk-averse, and a low UAI as being risk-seeking. Getting buy-in on a project—which is by definition unique and therefore prone to uncertainty—will be harder with high-UAI countries such as Greece, Portugal, and Guatemala, and easier with low UAI countries, such as Singapore, Jamaica, and Denmark. Change management in general will be easier in the low-UAI countries, because changes are often perceived as big buckets of uncertainty, which low-UAI countries can tolerate, even enjoy.

You can go to www.hofstede-insights.com/product/compare-countries/ to compare countries along these dimensions. You can see the striking difference between the United States and China in IDV and PDI, and even more so between Greece and China in UAI (Figure 8.2).

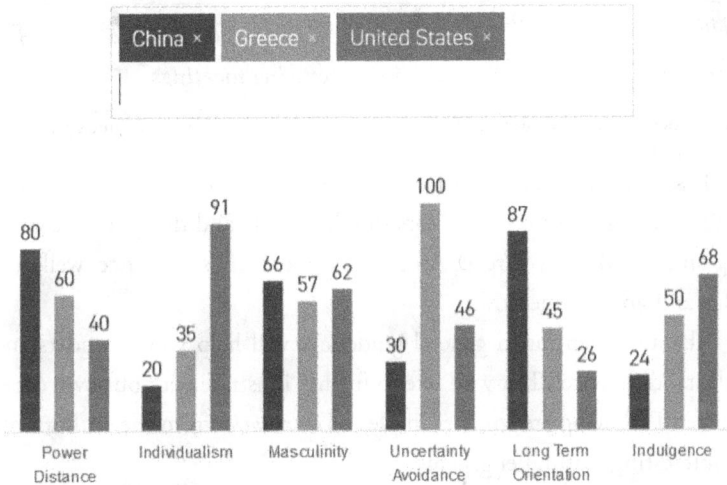

Figure 8.2 *Applying Hofstede's tool to compare national cultures*

Culture Dimensions and Project Planning Meetings

As mentioned, both authors have collaborated with people from India, China, and Finland on a fairly regular basis, to name just a few.

As this book is about meetings, we thought it would be interesting to first consider a chart that details how long it takes to start a meeting in various cultures (Figure 8.3). While there are some humorous elements to it, by and large, it has been confirmed to us, not only by our own experience but also by that of our students, that, yes, Germans start meetings right on time, and Latin countries tend to be more laid-back about starting times. Note that there is no right or wrong here.

Germany	▮	Formal introduction. Sit down. Begin.
Finland	▮	Formal introduction. Cup of coffee. Sit down. Begin.
US	▮	Informal introduction. Cup of coffee. Wisecrack. Begin.
UK	▬▬▬	Formal introduction. Cup of coffee and biscuits. 10 minutes small talk (weather, sport). Casual beginning.
France	▬▬▬▬▬	Formal introduction. 15 minutes small talk (politics, scandal, etc.). Begin.
Japan	▬▬▬▬▬▬	Formal introduction. Protocol seating. Green tea. 15-20 minutes small talk (humorous pleasantries). Sudden signal from senior Japanese. Begin.
Spain/ Italy	▬▬▬▬▬▬▬▬	20-30 minutes small talk (soccer, family matters) while others arrive. Begin when all there.

| Minutes | 0 | 5 | 10 | 15 | 20 | 25 | 30 |

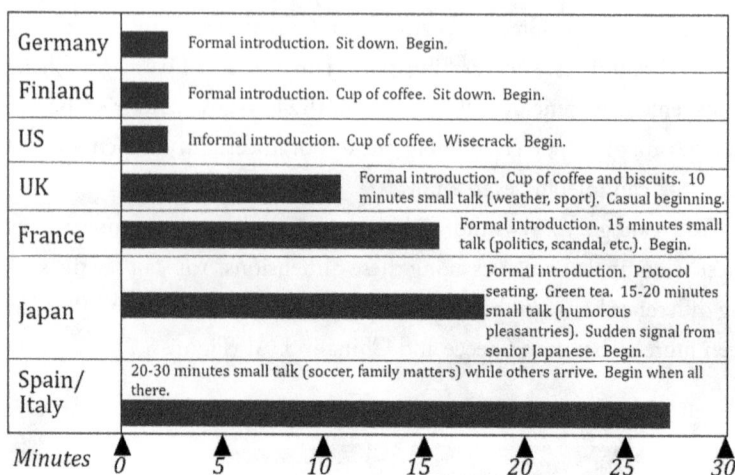

Figure 8.3 Cultural differences in structuring meetings

©2010 Richard D. Lewis, Richard Lewis Communications Ltd., www.crossculture.com.

Lesson learned? Account for differences. If you're an American holding a meeting in America, visitors should understand that you'll be starting on time. But if you're an American working in, say, France, well, just relax and go with the flow.

The aforementioned general guidelines will help you to understand cultural differences. But we'd like to further illustrate with our own experiences. Following are some examples of *war stories* from the authors' file of interesting cultural engagements.

The Thundering Table

One of us, attending his first meeting outside the United States, was tired after his first real international travel, and he finished his presentation somewhat bleary-eyed and waited for a reaction. He didn't have to wait long. He heard what sounded like a combination of thunder and amplified popping popcorn. The attendees were loudly pounding on the heavy wooden boardroom table. What had he done wrong to deserve this horrendous, disturbing, noise?

Nothing, it turns out. This is how a German audience expresses its appreciation for a good technical or academic presentation, a tradition that apparently started in German universities.

Dutch Directness Dares to Deliver Delightful Doom

One of us noted this sizeable cultural difference between the Dutch and the Americans while attending a risk planning meeting for a telecom network deployment. The Dutch attendees seemed to take great pleasure in identifying the threats—every single possible thing that could go wrong. To an American ear, it sounded like negativity. It sounded like the annual meeting of the Pessimists Club. (Not to be confused with the Procrastinators Club, which we haven't gotten around to joining.) After hearing all of these threats, he almost wanted to drop the project or, more accurately, run home, screaming in fear.

However, the exercise shifted to the opportunities (the things that could go horribly *right*), and the Dutch were equally adept at identifying these. When all was said and done, even with the long list of threats on the flipchart, in bright red ink, staring at the attendees, they couldn't wait to get to a local pub and celebrate the start of the project. So much for the Pessimists Club!

What the Dutch colleagues realized was that they had adequate levels of permission and safety (see our Deviled Eggs chapter) to act as full-fledged pessimists during the risk identification process, without fear of being called nay-sayers. They also demonstrated that it's possible, even advantageous, to shift attitudes, taking on the pessimist's viewpoint to identify what may go wrong, without losing optimism for the project. Remember—unidentified threats have zero chance of having any sort of planned risk response. Bottom line: The Dutch propensity for directness and risk aversion (noted by one author from two years in the Netherlands) is a good thing for risk identification during project planning meetings.

The Silent Treatment

One of us, after a fairly long and somewhat emotional presentation about sustainability in project management to a large Malaysian audience, was surprised at the near silence at the end of his presentation. Had he failed to convey the idea? Had he somehow insulted his audience? Why wasn't anyone asking any questions?

It turns out that in the Malaysian culture, the audience needs to be prompted and encouraged to respond. Luckily, the conference organizers were aware of this and had arranged for audio-visual assistants with microphones to wander through the audience and indicate that it was appropriate to ask questions. The presence of the people standing by with microphones was a living prompt for responses.

This turned the tide, and a dozen good-quality, well-thought-out questions were asked with increasing enthusiasm. This is reminiscent of the behavior of some Asian audiences at rock concerts, at which they'll sit quietly during the performance and then raucously applaud and celebrate at the conclusion.

Working With the Middle East Culture

One of us, who had never been to the Middle East or knew much about its culture beyond a surface level, was asked to set up a project management office for a company in Bahrain. Prior to engaging, he read up on Arabic culture in general, Bahraini in particular. A reliable source of information on this is the Richard Lewis book quoted earlier. He advises, for example, that "When introducing themselves, Westerners usually restrict the amount of information they give. Arabs tend to talk a lot about their family and connections."

He further states that "most Western countries have succeeded in creating equality for men and women. Arabs believe the two sexes have vastly different personalities and roles." But as to Bahrain specifically, Lewis says, "In Bahrain health and education programs are well-established, and women enjoy both university schooling and opportunities for a career."

So, the author was not surprised to find that in Bahrain, while his direct customer was a man and his two subordinates, the strategy team he interfaced with was comprised of several women who were every bit as demanding as the men. (There was some misunderstanding about why our intrepid author was hired, which it took most of the first meeting to clear up. But that's because the customer did not set expectations, on which we could write another whole book.)

The IT director and the author communicated frequently via WhatsApp and even met on Saturdays when the director had more time. The author found these unexpected sessions to be a lot more laid-back and provided an opportunity for the two to get to know each other as people. (The author, being leery of using the wrong hand signal, waited till the director would send him a thumbs-up on WhatsApp before responding in kind.)

Regarding our topic of meetings, when the author had to introduce the PMO concept to the project managers and strategy group, it was so quiet on Zoom you could hear a pin drop. Perhaps, he speculated, this was less fear of speaking up and more deference to the authority of the consultant (see power distance, in this chapter) about which he had been advised by the client.

The last thing to say here is that by and large, the project was successful, and despite our cultural differences, the author with his IT background could easily find common ground with the IT guys in Bahrain. Techies, one assumes, are more or less the same the world over. It also reinforces the idea that you need to consider both national and organizational culture.

Give or Take a Couple of Students

One of us taught a project management course at a university in the Liaoning Province of China. This was to be a two-weekend class, taught on Friday night and all day on Saturday and Sunday.

On arrival at the airport on Thursday, an assistant dean picked him up in a university van to take him to the hotel and brief him on the final course logistics. "There's some major construction at the building in which you'll be teaching," she said.

In fact, there's a three-meter-deep trench dug all the way around the building, with no fences, signs, or lighting. You're teaching on Friday night; it will be very dark. Do you want to hold the class? We may lose a student or two.

This was said without humor. It was a serious question. Aghast, he said, "No! We'll extend the Saturday and Sunday classes and teach through lunch." He remembered that the culture in China is much less risk-averse than in the United States, where that statement about losing a student or two would have made a great joke. This shows the value of understanding cultural differences.

Bowling for Business

One of us took an extensive course in Japanese language and culture. In the course, the instructor stressed the importance of your business card and the ceremonial nature of your *presentation* of the business card—we were strongly advised that when you do so, you're handing your colleague your essence or face (as in saving face), so you must do it in a specific way. There's even a name for it—*meishi koukan* (名刺交換). See our references for a description of this fascinating tradition.

Some of the students from the course visited Japan, and their first meeting was in a large, elongated room with a highly polished mahogany table. The American attendees entered on one side, and their Japanese colleagues on the other. Seeing the long, polished table, one of the Americans, despite all the coaching he'd received, simply couldn't resist the temptation, and flung his card, bowling style, along the table. It was thrown skillfully and skimmed easily almost the full length of the room.

My instructor, who was also attending, nearly fainted. She said it was as if the person had hurled *himself*, like a rather indelicate human bowling ball, on the table and slid head-first toward his Japanese hosts, who now were feeling a bit like bowling pins. There was no laughing—this was a cultural *faux pas* for sure, and the colleague got a strong reprimand from our instructor, and she came away with a very good story. And so did your authors!

195 Countries Separated by a Common Language

One of us ran an IT project wherein his job was to oversee the deployment of software and hardware for an investment bank in New York City. He had to communicate regularly with different parts of the country and with a few stakeholders in the United Kingdom. He was just starting to develop a relationship with a UK businessperson, and one day, during a phone call, they decided that a particular activity either was no longer needed or could be dismissed. Your intrepid author said, "Well then, let's just blow it off." ("Blow it off" is American slang for "let's avoid it" or "let's just not do it since it's not important.")

"Do *what*?" the Brit said. Realizing that he'd used an American expression, the author tried to explain what it meant. Once the Brit understood its meaning, he calmed down a little. But his subsequent words still resonate—"Never use that expression again," he said. Clearly, he found it somewhat offensive and highly colloquial. So, lesson learned.

This works both ways.

The other one of us was debriefing after a project meeting, and his colleague in the United Kingdom said, "Well, Kathrine was quite stroppy in the meeting, wasn't she?" "Stroppy?" he said. "What does that mean?" "Oh, you don't know? That means easily angered . . . irritable . . . that sort of thing." Even though he's an American of rather advanced age with decades of international work experience, he had never once heard that word used.

These are examples of people from two English-speaking countries. But culture is not just national but regional. In the United States, Southern and Northern culture are very different. People in the South tend to be more outgoing and friendlier in general. People in, say, New England tend to be more reserved. Consequently, Southerners might come away with the impression that New Englanders (or for that matter, anyone from the Northeastern United State) are unfriendly or rude. No, we just tend to keep to ourselves, and it's harder to get to know us.

You can imagine that for people with English as a second (or even third) language, the chance for such expressions to confound communications is orders of magnitude higher. Pay attention to your use of colloquialisms. Take an extra moment to be sure that you're using language that will easily cross borders without making your attendees stroppy. And don't blow it off!

Summary

We live in a multinational, multicultural world, and project managers are often asked to either work remotely with other cultures or travel to those sites. Regardless of one's national culture or background, it is not for us to go to other cultures and impose our ways on them. Not only will it not work, but it is also just the wrong thing to do.

It is incumbent on the project leader and team members to be aware of and sensitive to culture differences so that they do not create new issues that could have been avoided.

That said, don't just rely on any book. Talk to people in the culture, to those who have visited recently. Both authors were involved in a training for a European culture whose reputation is one of punctuality, dedication to learning, and precision. We found none of these things among the students. On questioning this with the manager who hired us, he said "Not anymore."

References

Hofstede Insights Organisational Culture Consulting. November 11, 2022. *Hofstede Insights*. www.hofstede-insights.com/ (accessed April 2, 2023).

Japanese business card ceremony: *meishi koukan*: https://blog.gaijinpot.com/exchanging-business-cards-japan/.

Lewis, R.D. n.d. *When Cultures Collide: Leading Across Cultures*, p. 401. Quercus. Kindle Edition.

New York Times: Inside Uber's Aggressive, Unrestrained Workplace Culture— www.nytimes.com/2017/02/22/technology/uber-workplace-culture.html.

www.redtangerine.org/cross-cultural-training/.

CHAPTER 9

Virtual Meetings

Key Takeaways

- 🐾 We now live in a highly virtual distributed world, and project success may entirely depend on your ability to navigate those waters.
- 🐾 Maintain your in-person large and in-charge stance.
- 🐾 Understand the tools that are available and become proficient in them.
- 🐾 Be aware that virtual meetings are more challenging due to the lack of physical presence and ability to read body language.
- 🐾 Respect those team members who do not want to go on camera.

The authors are indebted to Wayne Turmel on whose work this chapter was written. Wayne has spent over 15 years in the remote work and communication space. He's the cofounder of The Remote Leadership Institute and the cofounder of *The Long-Distance Leader, Rules for Remarkable Remote Leadership*. He's also (so he says) a pretty good guy once you get to know him.

Wayne's findings from the Remote Leadership Institute tell us:

- There's no way to avoid a learning curve, but it's worth it because the virtual meeting platforms do add value.
- It does take repeated use of the tools for them to become muscle memory, but when that happens, you can focus on the really important tasks and your role as a project leader.

Although we provide these tips, don't let yourself get overly hung up on the virtual piece. Get hung up *just enough*. Get set up and test and validate your system, which will prevent you from worrying about the webcam, background, and audio problems. If you have a compelling, well-facilitated meeting, you won't waste mental energy wondering if the people who aren't in the conference room with you are paying attention, answering e-mail, or getting to the next level on Wordle. (Which your authors play and compare notes on regularly. We have greatly expanded our five-letter vocabulary, often pulling them out of the clear azure.)

Note: While this book is pointedly not designed to be a postpandemic book, we do live in a postpandemic world. So, we think we need to acknowledge that the world has changed, and that employees are increasingly working from home or in hybrid (e.g., three days in office, two days at home, etc.) situations. So, all the more reason to know how to run a virtual meeting effectively. We aim to answer this question in the chapter: What do I need to do as the meeting leader before, during, and after the meeting to ensure success?

Quick Summary for Running Any Type of Virtual Meeting

We understand the concept of too long didn't read (TL; DR).

This chapter has a lot of detailed information, including the context and even science behind running successful virtual meetings. We've placed abbreviated versions of the top tips next for your convenience.

- Think about what type of meeting it is. The type of meeting—kickoff, update, lessons learned/retrospective, status, or collaboration—should determine the approach and tools.
- Visualize your virtual meeting underway and the action it generates 15 minutes after it's over and build that into your planning.

- Discover and use the technology that can help you win the battle over distance. Much of this chapter will focus on this aspect.
- Try out the technology beforehand so that you are not using it for the first time with *live* victims. Think Harry Potter—be sure your wizardry works before waving your wand!
- Secure your session with passwords, waiting rooms, and so on. Being Zoom bombed is not fun.
- Set a video and audio example! Be sure you look and sound as good as possible. Others will follow your lead.
- Consider starting longer meetings with an icebreaker. It could be anything from a round of introductions to a (hopefully) fun game.
- Understand and respect the fact that others may not want to be on camera.
- Monitor the chat and raised hands proactively. Make the meeting as inclusive as possible.
- Use built-in capabilities of the virtual platforms like whiteboards and polling.
- Use external tools such as Miro, Loom, Mural, and Google Jamboard, as appropriate to facilitate collaboration meetings.
- Set the rules early, reinforce them often, and show them you mean it. Demonstrate them yourself through your own behaviors just as you would with a face-to-face meeting.
- Avoid closed-ended questions. "How do you feel about this?" is scads better than, "All of you agree, right?"
- Record the meeting *if you receive everyone's permission.* Much information can be gleaned—by you as well as other stakeholders—with an ability to go back and listen and/or watch a second time.
- Be sure you have an accessible repository for all files (e.g., SharePoint, Dropbox, and Google Drive).
- Turn off any popups before sharing your screen.
- Be aware of Zoom fatigue and how to deal with it.

War Story—Computers 2, Humans 0

We do a good amount of project management training. Since the pandemic, it's all been virtual, and we try to use various features of technology, such as breakout rooms. One of the project managers was holding a training session and put her students into a breakout room. Or so she thought. Next thing she knew, she was trapped in a breakout room alone, and the rest of the class was in the main meeting. She was confused and ended the call, which forced everyone to log back in.

Another time, a PM was recording training for asynchronous training. She recorded the whole session and sent to our training specialist who was collecting the recordings for a program. The specialist watched it and realized quickly that the audio was never turned on. The PM had to rerecord the whole session. Lesson learned: Practice, practice, practice isn't just a mantra. It's key to successful meetings. Make sure you understand how to use technology prior to the meeting.

—Deb Cote, Senior Director of Planning
and Performance at a major hospital

War Story—Welcome to My World

I was contracting on a project for the real estate division of a financial company. My manager—who was a tough bird—and I had a virtual meeting with a product owner. During the course of the call, it was clear there was a disconnect between the product owner and the manager.

I had been sharing my screen to demonstrate some functionality. When the manager made yet another challenging statement, I could almost see the product owner rolling her eyes. I chatted "Welcome to my world" to her, completely forgetting that I was screen sharing, and that the manager could see that comment.

"What do you mean by welcome to my world?" she said. Recovering quickly, I laughed and said I was referring to the frustrations of our project and not specifically to her. She bought it, thankfully.

> It was actually kind of a dumb thing to do on my part. I will say that otherwise she and I had a good working relationship.
>
> —Jim Stewart

The New Reality—Virtual Meetings

When the COVID-19 pandemic forced many people to work from home in 2020, the world of work was forever altered. There were fewer in-person meetings and more web sessions using all kinds of tools. At the time, Zoom was mostly a free product (for up to 40 minutes) with little corporate penetration. In two years, it went from a niche ("What is Zoom?") to a verb (to Zoom) to a syndrome to "I cannot take one more Zoom call!" (Zoom doom.)

Our informal research and personal experience tell us that the number of meetings increased by at least 200 percent over the years between 2020 and 2022, some of it to enable productivity, some just to give people contact with their peers and colleagues. Whether this is a good thing or not, a general feeling arose that we now have too many meetings. Well, we have *always* had too many meetings, but now … wow! And they are back-to-back. Given our distributed world of work, it's more important than ever that when we hold meetings, they are (or at least *can* be) meaningful and productive—and move project work forward.

Virtual meetings are no longer just for kickoffs, status, or resolving issues. Increasingly, given the remoteness of team members from each other, they are for collaboration, for working together toward some common goal. So, in this chapter, we will address each of these types, take into consideration the overlaps, and provide examples of tools that you might use for each.

Preparing for a Virtual Meeting

The trick—just as it is for in-person meetings—is to *plan your meeting first*, using this book's guidance on knowing your intent, audience, and purpose, and *then* applying the technology as best you can to eliminate, mitigate, or at least do the best you can to overcome any challenges posed by distance.

If we're going to think this way, we need to consider our meetings in the following order. You won't be surprised to see these are the exact same things we (should) consider before *any* meeting:

- What are we trying to accomplish? What do we want participants to do/contribute/walk away with?
- What tools are at our disposal to accomplish these goals?
- What do I need to do as the meeting leader before, during, and after the meeting to ensure success?
- How will I know that the meeting is successful (see first bullet)?
- How can I be sure I keep people engaged during the virtual meeting?

What Are You Trying to Accomplish?

As form follows function, we must start with the simple question, "what are we trying to accomplish?" Any good project meeting has the same components. You want to deliver information in a way that's easily understood, answer questions, and help the team form (if they don't already know each other). You also want to allow for questions so that everyone understands their roles, goals, and duties, but also so that you also have a reasonable amount of faith that they get it.

So, what should we do to accomplish this goal? Communication, as you know, is more than a one-way transmission. For communication to occur, the message must be sent, received, and understood. We need a way to transmit information in as many ways as possible (visual, verbal, vocal—as in any communication situation), *and* to receive feedback in as many ways as possible. Now, how will you accomplish that in a virtual environment, where subtle, but important feedback cues (e.g., body language) are hidden or subdued?

Understanding the Tools at Your Disposal

We said earlier that virtual meetings are, first and foremost just meetings that are held when people are not all present in the same room.

Technology is merely another constraint among many you'll face on your project. The good news is that you probably have (or have access to) most of the tools you'll need. The bad (but fixable) news is you may not know of these tools or how to take advantage of them.

It probably won't surprise you that our informal research shows that 80 percent of people who use tools such as Zoom; Microsoft Teams or WebEx use only 20 percent of the features. That's economist Vilfredo Pareto and his 80/20 principle at it again! (Pareto showed that approximately 80 percent of the land in Italy was owned by 20 percent of the population.) In project work, that's fairly surprising, given that we tend to be tech and process-oriented people to start with. Still, we're human, and pragmatic (lazy, even) and tend to use only as much of a given technology as we *think* we need to get the job done. This may also be a symptom of the folks at Zoom or Microsoft Teams just developing features because, well, feature development is what they do.

In any event, part of the problem is that according to our informal research over 70 percent of users wind up using these tools for the first time in front of live victims (we use that word quite intentionally—they will suffer along with you if you struggle). We don't get any training or coaching on the presentation platform other than to fire it up and do the bare minimum. We learn from watching others give presentations. The problem is we've never seen most of the tools used in the context of a good meeting. Why would we think about applying them in a broader way?

At first, this seems counterintuitive. After all, there are a lot of web meeting and presentation platforms out there. If you don't know how to use Zoom or Teams, for example, how are you supposed to be effective? The good news is that they all offer approximately the same general functionality. The best analogy is renting a car. You may not know how to turn the headlights on for that exact model, but you're pretty sure this car has them, and you just need to know where that darned button, switch, or lever is. (And it's not likely you will have to crawl under the car to get to the gas cap.)

Still, it cannot hurt—and can only help—to ask the rental agent, "Are there any quirks to the controls or displays of this car that I should know about?"

Before we delve deeper into technology, we also need to acknowledge there are three ways to distinguish virtual and in-person meetings, and they each have their own challenges:

- The entirely in-person meeting: everyone's in the same room at the same time. We have a professional lifetime of experience with these (which doesn't mean we're good at them), but at least we have the advantage of being all together at the same time, getting the messages unfiltered, benefitting from unconscious nonverbal signals, and allowing free, fast-moving communication.
- The entirely virtual meeting: We are limited by the platform we're using, but at least in a virtual meeting everyone is on WebEx, Zoom, or Teams and has equal access to the platform and (in the right hands) an equal ability to take part. Nobody has an advantage over anyone else, and all are equally miserable.
- The hybrid meeting: If you've ever been in that meeting where some people are in the conference room and the rest are connected to a squawky speaker phone, you are familiar with these. Some people are having the live experience, others are at the mercy of technology and a lack of visibility. One of us was recently at a meeting in which the presenter was online as well, so he was both online *and* in-person! There are some interesting interpersonal dynamics here. Ignore them at your peril.

But as we're letting form follow function, let's put this whole technology discussion into context. Specifically, what are we trying to do, and how can the tools help (or hinder) our effectiveness?

What's the *Function* That Form Follows?

If we quickly list the things that need to happen for any meeting to be successful, you will see that it doesn't matter much whether that meeting is online or in Conference Room B. For each goal of the meeting, there are multiple ways to achieve that goal. The trick is to find the closest feature or function that allows us to achieve that goal as effectively as possible in a virtual environment.

For example, when we ask people, "what would you do in an entirely in-person meeting to get input?," they might say something like, "ask for a show of hands." In a conference room, everyone knows to raise their hand. Most virtual platforms have a *raise hand* feature, or some other way of making themselves known. If you or your team don't know how to use it, that's a tool that levels the playing field, so use it, to have the function follow the form!

So, what are trying to do in our meeting? Again, it depends on the type of meeting, but here's a list showing what we think you would want to accomplish:

- Help everyone on the team get to know the leaders, stakeholders—and each other (kickoff meeting)
- Deliver information in a multitude of ways and media so that people really understand what the project is (big picture) and their role in it (individual tasks and roles)
- Make important decisions using informed data
- Answer any questions or objections people may have
- Collaborate to create project artifacts, processes, team norms, and action items
- Ensure understanding and buy-in
- Leave people feeling energized, positive, and with some of their will to live intact

Helping Everyone Get to Know Each Other—the Details

As you know (but it's worth repeating here), a team is only as good as the working relationships between its members. The kickoff is often the first (often one of the few) opportunities for everyone to get to know who they're working with. We need to have as full an experience of each other as possible. That means visual, vocal, and verbal communication. If the team in Bangalore is simply a list of names to the team in Boston, you're beginning the working relationship at a disadvantage.

Recalling our form follows function idea, consider this: in a live meeting, you can go around the room and everyone gets to introduce themselves. We can see each other, hear one another, joke, laugh, and get to know our teammates. In a virtual meeting, you have the opportunity to use webcams and other ways for people to interact, and in a hybrid meeting, you may or may not have the ability for everyone to make an equally good first impression on each other. Consider these things when it comes to your meeting objective of making sure that people are getting to meet each other regardless of the meeting format (in-person, hybrid, and virtual).

For his remote classes, one of the authors has experimented with the following: prior to the session, ask each person to put together a one- or two slide PowerPoint. Each attendee can use that brief presentation (with visuals) to introduce herself, her family, hobbies, and so on. It's a nice way to break the ice and perhaps find some commonality. (Seemingly everyone has a dog or cat they love to gush over.)

The other thing to acknowledge is diverse personality types. Some people are extraverts, some are introverts. Some will come on camera without hesitation, some cannot be coaxed to for a million bucks. (Or 952,444 €, 1,326,460,00.00 ¥—you get the idea.) What do you do in these situations?

Well, first it's important to treat everyone with respect. And so, trying to get someone to turn their camera on when they really don't want to is going to create more resistance than just letting it go. Think about it—do you see people when you're on the phone with them? Actually, these days, perhaps you do—but certainly not all the time. Allow people to have a *bad hair* day.

As you progress, it is somewhat less important that every member of the team be on camera all the time (it might be lunch time in Prague and nobody needs to see Tomás enjoy his sandwich), but the smaller the group, the more power visual connection has. One-on-one meetings and small groups really benefit from the ability to see each other's faces.

We think that breaking the ice is critically important at a virtual meeting—and it is a bit different than in an in-person meeting. Consider that some of your speakers may have English as a second language (assuming you are using English as your meeting language), and that may mean they are less willing to speak up. Often breakout rooms can help, as some people are more comfortable working and speaking up in small groups as opposed to a crowd (a flock? a gaggle? a coven?) of 35 people.

Take advantage of the chat features of virtual meeting platforms, you may find that you are now getting people who were shy about talking are quite a bit more talkative. It will allow those who may be shy about speaking (or even those with a sore throat!) to convey their thoughts and to actively participate.

For More Effective Virtual Meetings, Set the Rules and Expectations

Set the rules for your virtual meeting and show them you mean it. Meeting behavior is often a result of conditioning. People can get accustomed to going to meetings and not truly being present (attentive, interested, and participative). Be sure that you (yes, you) are following the rules you've set.

Demonstrating the preferred behaviors will help reinforce them. It's not just rules—set expectations early (examples: we expect everyone to introduce themselves, ask questions when you have them—don't wait, every team member is expected to contribute to the discussion). Let participants know upfront that you will periodically call on people, give them a chance to contribute, and allow them to do it in a way that's comfortable for them.

War Story—Are We There Yet?

I work on medical information reporting systems. We had a meeting that was meant to allow our medical staff to give feedback on new features we developed for them. We worked hard on these features to provide better efficiency and workflow. At the meeting, we expected the medical staff representative to review and ask for even further features, representing how they really work.

I finished the presentation and demo of the features, expecting feedback. At the end of my presentation, the representative said, rather abruptly, "Are we done? ... great!" and started out the door. Aghast, I said, "umm, we were waiting for your thoughts on this."

She said, "Mmm …. I don't think we need these features at all, to say nothing of adding even more."

We looked at each other, simultaneously surprised and disappointed. In fact, at first, I thought it was a joke.

But it wasn't a joke. We felt like our effort was wasted.

Lesson learned! We avoid this moving forward by setting meeting expectations properly upfront and assuring the right attendees are there.

—Mirela Andoni, healthcare PM, former student, via LinkedIn

Technical Advice for Virtual Meetings

Be sure that participants can see each other. Our brains crave visual connection. The most powerful way of introducing each other is to be sure that people connect a face with a voice and a role. In person, this happens automatically. Online, we need to take advantage of webcams and video conferencing (with the caveats from above in place). It doesn't have to be high-tech Cisco Telepresence (although that's lovely). A simple webcam (assuming you can actually see the person, and they aren't backlit like they're in Witness Protection) will do. If that is impossible, at least have photographs of participants you can share with the team.

If your built-in camera isn't good, consider getting an external one whose quality is often higher. The price for a good-quality webcam (and microphone) has come way down. Set these expectations (of good quality video and audio) before the call and hold people accountable for the quality of their appearance in your meetings. If you're an IT person overseeing equipment for home use, consider bulk purchases of good-quality cameras and microphones for those who will be participating from remote locations.

Your appearance is key, not just for you but as an example, set up your webcam at eye level. You don't want to give people the impression you're looking down your nose at them—nor does your audience want to look up your nose. Show your shoulders and your face and don't be too close to the camera or too far away. You want a nice contrast, not too dark, not too bright. Ideally you can use a light that allows you to increase or decrease the intensity.

A window to provide natural light is useful (but not directly behind you). So are a couple of soft, diffused side lights so that you are not half in dark, half in light like some evil villain from the *Batman* franchise. Approach it as a photographer would. Ask a friend to check it out with you. Note that in a pinch, you can use your mobile camera for your Zoom calls. You'll have to download an app such Droidcam or Epoccam, and then buy a small, inexpensive tripod to mount it. It's an alternative to an external camera.

If you're using the audio through your web platform, headsets and microphones are a must. As mentioned, for U.S.$100 to U.S.$200, studio-quality USB microphones are available and the full richness of a person's voice can come through. A professional tip: keep your lips about 7 to 8 inches (18 cm) from the front surface of the microphone. You can even use the Hawaiian *shaka sign*, you know, the one that surfers use, with pinkie and thumb extended, to gauge that distance. If you've got a good built-in microphone, great. But keep a good headset nearby just in case—as is the situation with one of us—your neighbor has their lawn loudly landscaped seemingly every 15 minutes. Test your audio as we suggested—with a friend—before the meeting.

Let's talk audio for a moment. One common mistake people make is to automatically mute everyone who isn't in the room. (And let's face it, they're the ones who need muting, more often than not.) This (perhaps unintentionally) sends the subliminal message that anyone remote is less important than anyone else, and it will require more work to get them to contribute, because they've, in effect, been told to be quiet and don't speak unless spoken to.

If at all possible, allow them the choice of muting themselves or not. Be very clear that their input is desired and valued, and that they can unmute themselves at will. If they have background issues (barking dogs, crying coworkers, city sirens), they can turn off their mics, but make it clear that mic-muting is not equivalent to permission to fade into the background.

Be sure that those tuning in remotely have good audio. Try to avoid people who have dialed in via a cellphone in remote Outer Granbia.*

---

* This is a reference to a very real, very small town in rural western Massachusetts, named Granby—and we just like how *Outer Granbia* sounds. And again because it makes us chuckle.

If both parties are using speakerphones or smartphones on the speaker setting, you have a recipe for bad connections, garbled audio, and an audience that tunes out.

Have a *Plan B* room you can run to just in case your Plan A room is unavailable. In a pinch, you can use your kitchen with the barking dogs. We're all used to that postpandemic. Just don't make a habit of it. One of us recently attended a meeting where a woman was holding a newborn baby. Everyone understood.

Additional Tips to Be Better Prepared for a Virtual Meeting

Before you enter a virtual meeting, think of everything that could go wrong. If you're using, say, a Windows PC and you've been using it all day, you might have chewed up a lot of memory. In that case, before you go remote, consider rebooting, and/or using a PC accessory like Wise-Cleaner (www.wisecleaner.com). This often solves a host of problems. It will give you memory back, and you'll experience greater speed and fewer problems. (Same applies for a mobile phone.)

Check your background (what's behind you in the room, in fact, or via a false background). Don't have a background that is so compelling to look at so that people are trying to find out what books you read. One of us has a (rather boring) background that has a lamp and a painting of a sunflower. But it provides at least a minimum of visual interest and color. if you're smart, let it come through in the way you present yourself not because you have a copy of *On Being and Nothingness* on your bookshelf.

Check your background before you start. Perhaps the last time you used Zoom, you created a fun background for your five-year-old niece's birthday party. If you join the meeting with animated *My Little Pony* icons floating around, you may not be giving out the serious vibe you wanted for your meeting with that federal authority that is auditing your organization. Remember that guy who went to a court hearing and had an avatar that looked like a cat? You don't want to be him.

Unless you have a good green screen, beware the virtual background. If you move your arms around or want to hold up something like a book, spots of transparency occur, and it just looks weird. If you're going to be sharing your screen, turn off or pause notifications on anything that might cause a popup—Facebook, Slack, Dropbox, your e-mail software, LinkedIn job notifications, and so on. Close windows for any websites up that you don't want anyone to see, even if it's just your calendar. People will fixate on that, and you could trigger questions in their mind that are irrelevant, distracting, or even damaging. ("Hmm, she has a dentist appointment and has an appointment with a competitor....")

Consider turning off your self-view. Think about it. When you talk to people in person, are you seeing yourself at the same time? No, that would be unnatural. Once everything looks good, turn off your self-view. You can kick it back on once in a while just to double-check that you're not slouching down in your chair.

Set meeting permissions for maximum collaboration before the meeting starts. Most platforms allow you to control the amount of interaction in a meeting, who can chat with whom, who can present content, who can write on the whiteboard, and so on. Decide early on what you want people to do during the meeting and set those permissions before the meeting starts. You don't have to think too hard about it in the moment, and it sends a subtle message that passive attendance isn't expected or appreciated.

Be sure the participant list is visible. Knowing who's on the call at all times is really helpful. Who haven't you heard from yet? Who do you know that has knowledge worth sharing? One huge advantage of virtual meetings over conference calls or video conferencing is you have a reminder of who's there. You can also send private chat messages directly from the participant list. But be prepared to shut that down if people are getting distracted with side conversations.

Record the meeting. It's entirely likely that your whole team won't make the meeting. *With permission*, use the recording feature to ensure that stragglers, latecomers, dilly-dalliers, and those who were legitimately late due to putting out fires, have the same chance to know their teammates, hear the discussion, and hear the same information the same way as everyone else. Also, when people know they're being recorded (as above—with permission), there is no room for "oh, I didn't commit to that." Note—Under the U.S. Electronic Communications Privacy Act of 1986 (ECPA), it is *against the law* to record a conversation without consent from at least one party (depending on the state).

We like the idea of assigning a chat deputy to keep track of visual and audio distractions and to bring those to the leader's attention—let them know that someone is trying to contribute or ask a question, or needs to mute their microphone or camera.

Use breakout rooms judiciously. In the past, breakout rooms were fraught with peril. No one was quite sure how to use them and you crossed your fingers and hoped they worked. But in recent years, it has become commonplace to use breakouts to assign people to different rooms to collaborate. This is something you'll want to experiment with before doing it in a larger meeting. But we've found that intelligent use of breakouts can be very rewarding. You can jump around from room to room, check in on how teams are doing, and set a timer for when they will return to the main room.

The authors have had great success using breakouts in their training and consultation sessions, having found this: before sending people off to their breakout rooms, check for understanding of the breakout task. It's all too commonplace to send people off to breakout rooms and have them come back saying, "We weren't sure what to do." Make sure it's clear as you send them off, and then go into those rooms one-by-one and be sure instructions are clear. Leave enough time for teams to work on exercises. It'll take them five minutes (at least) to figure out who's doing what.

Use chat proactively. Many meeting leaders try to limit chat because they find it distracting. For many people, it's a great way to get the best input from people. Some folks are shy and don't like to interrupt speakers to contribute by voice. As mentioned previously, those with English as a second language (or third, or fourth) often find it's easier to write out their thoughts than try to compete with accents and bad audio.

In the project world, the team may be full of introverts, or people who actually like to put a coherent thought together before just opening their mouths. Allow people to contribute in a way that's both comfortable and effective. If you're presenting a slide deck or are otherwise (temporarily, we hope!) in broadcast mode, take advantage of the chat deputy we mentioned above and empower them to interrupt you if a relevant question or comment comes along and needs immediate attention.

Gather information just as you would an entirely in-person meeting. As we mentioned earlier, we gather a lot of information during a meeting. "Who has experience with that customer?" "How many people have used Basecamp in the past?" Most tools have multiple ways of gathering information ranging from formal (polling and survey tools, emoticons, chat, or mark-up tools like checks or *XXs*) to a simple voice vote or show of hands, which can be done virtually as well. One could make an argument that virtual meeting platforms actually improve our ability to capture important meeting information—the simple fact that you can record the meeting is an example.

Be secure. One of us has attended two networking meetings—by the same group—that were Zoom bombed. The first one was funny. A guy came on and stuck a small electric razor up his nose. Dumb, but amusing.

The second one? Not so much. The bogus attendees used legitimate attendees' names to chat hateful racist messages. The meeting was totally hijacked, and we had to regroup in a new channel. It had been publicly advertised meeting, and one newcomer said he'd never come back. Use passwords and/or a waiting room. Check with the vendor or a cybersecurity expert in your company for ways to avoid this.

If all of this seems like too much overhead, consider alternatives to the virtual meeting. With time zones, flexible work schedules, and more, the best way to get good input from everyone may be to use asynchronous solutions (like Slack) for preliminary brainstorming and information gathering, then utilize your time together for the really meaty conversations. Another tool is called Loom (www.loom.com). Loom allows team members to record a brief video, for example, a how-to, and then share it with others via a link without requiring an account.

Virtual Is Only Part of the Meeting Problem—Some Advice From Wayne Turmel

There's a statistic that Wayne likes to share with people in his classes. It has two parts:

- Two-thirds of the time spent on virtual meetings (web meetings, videoconferences, and teleconferences) is considered wasted by attendees. But....
- The time considered wasted on *real* meetings is still 50 percent or more.

In other words, per Wayne (his words), meetings pretty much suck. Making them virtual just adds a bit to the general suckiness. There is some good news, though. Just as with proper planning, preparation, and facilitation your regular meetings can be more effective, the same is true with virtual meetings.

And it really doesn't matter what tools or platforms you use, as long as you use them effectively. Remember, Genghis Khan ruled half the known world and never held a single Zoom meeting. (Rumor has it he drove everyone crazy with text messages featuring axe emoticons, but the authors have found no archeological evidence of this.)

Speaking of Time Zones

As noted, both your authors teach, and when we do—and when we talk about virtual meetings and their challenges—one of the first ones to get mentioned frequently is time zones.

If you are based, for example, in the eastern United States, it is not at all uncommon to be collaborating with people on the west coast of the United States, in Thailand, in India, in Poland, Manitoba, Singapore, Japan, South Africa, and/or Australia. A recent colleague of ours found exactly one overlap in time among Central Europe and the East and West coasts of the United States. (He used Loom for short videos when he could not hold a workshop.)

So, the first problem is that you are occasionally going to be up at some weird hour. Or somebody is. If you're the project manager, as likely as not it will be *you* who has to bend a little. But there is no harm—and a sort of servant leadership aspect—in rotating the up at 5 a.m. or working till 10 p.m. shifts. You're a team, yes?

But firstly, you have to schedule the thing. And everybody—at least once—will make the mistake of e-mailing 37 people on the e-mail list and saying:

The meeting is at 11 a.m. on Zoom.

At which point, you will have created a veritable babel of confusion with everyone writing at the same time to establish which time zone you're talking about.

Try listing several time zones such as:

The meeting is at 11 a.m. EST USA, 10 a.m. CST USA, 9 a.m. PST USA, 9:30 p.m. Bangalore India. Also note the GMT.

Be sure that when you send the meeting request that your calendar is set on your time zone. It will, of course, adjust for others.

There are several tools you can use to help you avoid scheduling a meeting at a time that could be poor for all parties.

World Time Buddy is pretty handy. It's a convenient world clock, a time zone converter, and an online meeting scheduler. www.worldtime-buddy.com/. You can view multiple time zones at once, and a slider allows you to shift times to align them.

Time and Date also has a Meeting Planner (www.timeanddate.com/worldclock/meeting.html) function, which is exceedingly helpful. It uses color codes to show the best times. Red is really bad, bright green is really good, and shades of yellow indicate times that aren't great but will work.

For example, if you are in Boston, Massachusetts, and your colleagues are in Melbourne, Australia, Paris, France, and Cape Town, South Africa (see Figure 9.1), you can see the only possible time is Monday at 7 a.m. in Boston, unless you are an early bird, your colleague in Melbourne is a night owl. All other times have at least one city in red.

People are really funny about their calendars. It's okay if you mess up once and everybody shows up at the wrong time and place. Do it twice? You have a reputation. Not good.

Also, if you happen to be working outside an organization and want to show people your available time, having a Calendly calendar can't hurt. Calendly is an app for scheduling meetings. Its advantage is that it eliminates the problematic back-and-forth when trying to determine a time that makes sense for everyone. Rather than e-mail chains and phone tag, you send your availability with a Calendly link (even if the people booking time with you don't use Calendly).

Doodle is another tool for this purpose. Like Calendly, Doodle is a web-based scheduling tool that helps reduce the hassle of organizing meetings via e-mail or phone. (And it should be noted here that many

UTC-time	Boston	Melbourne	Paris	Cape Town
Monday, April 25, 2022 at 08:00:00	Mon 4:00 am *	Mon 6:00 pm	Mon 10:00 am *	Mon 10:00 am
Monday, April 25, 2022 at 09:00:00	Mon 5:00 am *	Mon 7:00 pm	Mon 11:00 am *	Mon 11:00 am
Monday, April 25, 2022 at 10:00:00	Mon 6:00 am *	Mon 8:00 pm	Mon 12:00 noon *	Mon 12:00 noon
Monday, April 25, 2022 at 11:00:00	Mon 7:00 am *	Mon 9:00 pm	Mon 1:00 pm *	Mon 1:00 pm
Monday, April 25, 2022 at 12:00:00	Mon 8:00 am *	Mon 10:00 pm	Mon 2:00 pm *	Mon 2:00 pm
Monday, April 25, 2022 at 13:00:00	Mon 9:00 am *	Mon 11:00 pm	Mon 3:00 pm *	Mon 3:00 pm
Monday, April 25, 2022 at 14:00:00	Mon 10:00 am *	Tue 12:00 midnight	Mon 4:00 pm *	Mon 4:00 pm
Monday, April 25, 2022 at 15:00:00	Mon 11:00 am *	Tue 1:00 am	Mon 5:00 pm *	Mon 5:00 pm
Monday, April 25, 2022 at 16:00:00	Mon 12:00 noon *	Tue 2:00 am	Mon 6:00 pm *	Mon 6:00 pm
Monday, April 25, 2022 at 17:00:00	Mon 1:00 pm *	Tue 3:00 am	Mon 7:00 pm *	Mon 7:00 pm
Monday, April 25, 2022 at 18:00:00	Mon 2:00 pm *	Tue 4:00 am	Mon 8:00 pm *	Mon 8:00 pm
Monday, April 25, 2022 at 19:00:00	Mon 3:00 pm *	Tue 5:00 am	Mon 9:00 pm *	Mon 9:00 pm
Monday, April 25, 2022 at 20:00:00	Mon 4:00 pm *	Tue 6:00 am	Mon 10:00 pm *	Mon 10:00 pm
Monday, April 25, 2022 at 21:00:00	Mon 5:00 pm *	Tue 7:00 am	Mon 11:00 pm *	Mon 11:00 pm

Figure 9.1 Let software help you avoid meeting time zone faux pas

Permission granted by Edward Angelo Cerullo (webmaster@timeanddate.com).

companies use Microsoft Outlook, which will advise of available times and account for time zone differences.)

https://calendly.com/

https://doodle.com/en/

Deliver Information in Multiple Ways

Meetings contain a lot of information. Some is in the form of collected data, while some will come as stories, told by experienced team members. The important thing to remember is that human beings intake information into our systems in multiple ways. A good meeting provides more than just one form of communication. After all, if you're just showing spreadsheet after spreadsheet, you may as well e-mail it out and save everyone the aggravation.

Here are some of the ways virtual meetings can help add value:

- Show as well as tell. As mentioned previously, people are visual creatures. We often need to view a bar chart rather than have someone tell us about a trend. Cynically, we also have the attention span of dogs (squirrel!) and having something to look at that supports the topic under discussion will help keep us focused on that, rather than our e-mail.
- Screen sharing is fine for showing spreadsheets or demonstrating software. If you will be showing a lot of information, though, consider uploading your content (PowerPoint, PDFs, etc.) so that you can quickly switch from one piece of information to another. Just as in a regular meeting, you can move from a PowerPoint presentation to the whiteboard, to a handout and back, uploading the content to the software (in Teams, check out the PowerPoint Live sharing option). It's less frustrating for everyone.
- Whiteboards are amazing for maintaining focus and communication. People retain information when they see it and hear it. By using a whiteboard or a flip chart in a traditional meeting, you can get the best of both worlds. Most platforms have whiteboard features that serve the

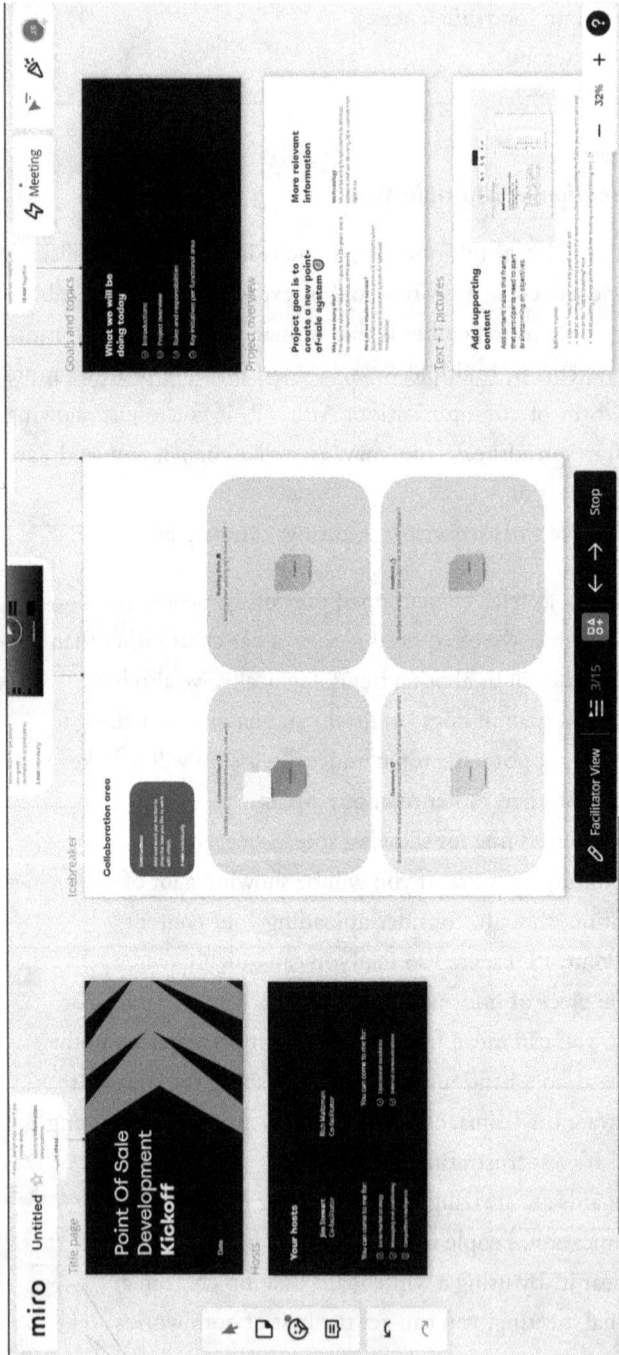

Figure 9.2 Miro Screenshot 1

same purpose. You can capture input from discussions and brainstorms, while leaving them up for visual reinforcement. You can also save the whiteboards from most web meeting tools. Many videoconferencing systems tie to smart whiteboards in the meeting room as well.

- Use collaborative tools. Tools like Miro, or Mural are constantly evolving and can create a dynamic, interactive environment where everyone can participate and add value. Typically, they allow for team members to not only see the big picture but also to collaborate using virtual Post-it Notes. Both authors have done work using stickies and for tactile feel they can't be beat. Using them virtually is the next best thing if you want to engage people.

Following is an example of Miro, which can be used for remote collaboration. Figure 9.2 is on the previous page shows an overview of the project. The collaborative piece in the center where virtual Post-It Notes can be used to share ideas is blown up in Figure 9.3.

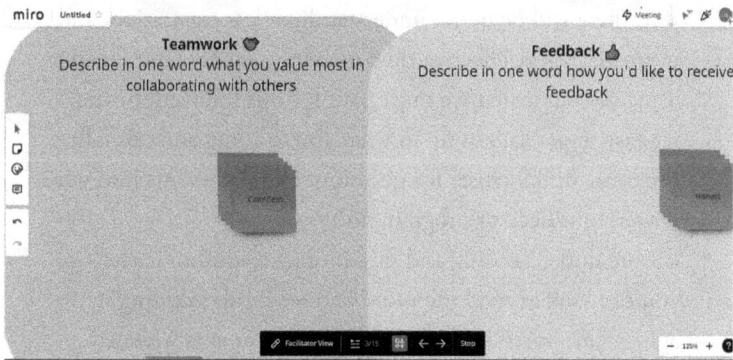

Figure 9.3 Miro Screenshot 2

Permission to use graphics granted by Miro.

- Smartsheet has a nifty product called Workapps, which allows you to create quick no-code applications. They have several templates, one of which is (fortuitously) called Meeting Management. It automatically creates forms such as *Meeting Agenda and Follow-up* and *Overdue Actions for Follow-Up.*

- Answer questions and objections anyone might have as quickly as possible.
- One of the most common—and most self-sabotaging— behaviors people exhibit in virtual meetings is to cram all the information in up front and ask people to hold their questions until the end. This isn't how people process information. In a regular meeting, you'd say something, look out at the audience, and see confusion, resistance, or understanding, and check in with them. Online, there's a tendency not to do that because we're not getting the visual cues. Be conscious of this. If, as meeting leader, you're going to be doing a lot of the talking, having that deputy around to remind you to check in with the audience from time to time is a good idea.
- During virtual meeting presentations, integrate the Q&A within the presentation rather than necessarily placing them at the end. You've been in meetings where someone outlines a three-step process, then calls for questions. Inevitably, the first question is, "can you go back to step one?" You'll find that if people can question or check for understanding along the way, there will be better understanding, less frustration, and ultimately more effective time management for your meeting. The problem is that we must plan for this interaction, and it's easy to get caught up in what you're doing and not take the time. Build pauses for questions and comments into your PowerPoint deck or program notes.
- Ensure understanding and buy-in. In a traditional meeting, you can look around the room and see heads nodding in agreement, bored looks of complacency, or eyes widened in panic. Those are important clues that tell you whether you can proceed with the meeting as planned, need to take a deeper dive into something, or skip ahead. Online you're missing many of those signs that people understand and buy-in to what's being said (or not.)
- Don't ask closed-ended questions. You'll notice a dramatic difference in the number of responses and the quality of input if you don't ask simple, closed questions like "any questions?" and replace them with more specific, open-ended queries.

"What else might get in the way of success?" is a very different question than, "anyone have anything else?" Again, gain both oral and written input.

What If the Virtual Meeting Isn't Going Well?

What you then do depends on how badly it's going and whether or not it makes more sense to continue or to call it a day and regroup later. Case in point—one of us was working on a project to roll out a new resource management and time tracking software. Going into the meeting, we were warned that people were not happy that they would have a second method of time tracking for a period of time, no matter the benefit.

It in fact turned out that one of the teams had just introduced Agile (with Jira) and now they would have to use a *third* method of time tracking. Needless to say, this was not well received by the troops. People were not angry so much as frustrated. We could have canceled the call and held it another day. But we kept it going for at least 15 minutes past the meeting's scheduled time and heard everyone out. As a result, not only did we *not* deploy the third method, but we also began a discussion on how to integrate these various methods. The meeting started dismally, but we were able to pivot it to positive postmeeting action.

For the record, while most participants' cameras were off, the author left his on the whole time. This was intentional as it was *his* meeting. And even when the going got rough, he wanted to show that he was still cool, calm, and collected (at least on the outside), and that this was just another issue to be dealt, with not something to panic over or hide from.

And if you're curious as to the outcome of this scenario, we shelved the idea of doing multiple time tracking. Initially. But someone upstairs wanted it done, and so while the author has since moved on, his understanding is that one way or the other, it will eventually happen.

Leave People Feeling Energized and Positive

This is more of a mindset issue than a technical one. As you've doubtless heard so many times, you only get one chance to make a first impression. If people feel like they've been on a death march, the project will not get off to a positive, energetic start. If, on the other hand, people believe their time was well spent, their initial questions are answered, they will be heard as the project continues, and the leader (that's you) knows what they're doing.

Make a point of saying, out loud, how thankful you are for their participation and hard work. And keep saying it till they believe you. This isn't a technology thing, but with virtual meetings, it's hard to stay focused and engaged. When people put the effort in, it should be acknowledged. That way, there's a better than even shot they'll stay that way for the next meeting as well.

Does Virtual Work Hinder Creativity?

An interesting study was published in the April 2022 issue of *Nature* Magazine that indicated that Zoom (or, one assumes, other remote methods of meeting) hinders creativity. It doesn't prevent it—it *hinders* it. But according to the study—for which 600 people were recruited—there were some compelling findings.

- In-person meetings generate more ideas—and more creative ones—compared with videoconferencing. However, interestingly…
- Choosing which idea to then pursue wasn't hindered by videoconferencing

What leads to these fascinating findings? It turns out that in a virtual meeting, everyone, not surprisingly, is focused on their screens and not the environment. According to the study,

> …in-person teams operate in a fully shared physical space, whereas virtual teams inhabit a virtual space that is bounded by the screen in front of each member. Our data suggest that this physical difference in shared space compels virtual communicators to narrow their visual field by concentrating on the screen and filtering out peripheral visual stimuli that are not visible or relevant to their partner and as virtual communicators narrow their visual scope to the shared environment of a screen, their cognitive focus narrows

in turn. This narrowed focus constrains the associative process underlying idea generation, whereby thoughts "branch out" and activate disparate information that is then combined to form new ideas.

Take a moment and think about the fact that a project, by definition, is an endeavor undertaken to produce a unique product, service, or outcome (keyword being unique). That means, you and your team need creativity, and anything that augments it is valuable to your project.

Even movement—as that study indicates—can stimulate ideas. As we noted in our Preface, Steve Jobs was famous for taking long walks when he wanted to think something through. "Staying still hinders creativity," says Jeremy Bailenson, founding director of the Stanford Virtual Human Interaction Lab (VHIL).

As a case in point, General Electric moved their headquarters to Boston a few years ago, in part so they could get the kind of in-person communication in an innovative area (Boston is home to about 40 universities and colleges and many high-tech and biomedical firms) where they might just bump into someone or meet them at a coffee house. Silicon Valley has thrived in this fashion as well.

As to choosing which idea to pursue, as noted, video conferencing seemed to have no appreciable impact that. Perhaps because that's A versus B task as opposed to idea creation.

Consider this in planning your virtual meetings. You may simply ask people to mute their video and look around—perhaps even *walk* around—their home office when brainstorming. You can find some excellent tips (in general) as to how to deal with the cognitive load of virtual meetings here: www.thegrove.com/blog/9-tips-for-lightening-the-load-of-zoom-fatigue.

A Brief Word on Zoom Fatigue

Ever since Zoom became not only popular but almost *de rigeur* in early 2020, the concept of Zoom fatigue started to surface. In an article called *Stanford researchers identify four causes for "Zoom fatigue" and their simple fixes*, Professor Jeremy Bailenson examined the psychological consequences of spending hours per day on these platforms. Much of it buttresses our arguments and advice.

1. Excessive amounts of close-up eye contact are highly intense.
   Both the amount of eye contact we engage in on video chats, as well as the size of faces on screens are unnatural. In a normal meeting, people will variously be looking at the speaker, taking notes, or looking elsewhere. But on Zoom calls, everyone is looking at everyone, all the time.

   Solution: Until the platforms change their interface, Bailenson recommends taking Zoom out of the full-screen option and reducing the size of the Zoom window relative to the monitor to minimize face size, and to use an external keyboard to allow an increase in the personal space bubble between oneself and the grid.

2. Seeing yourself during video chats constantly in real time is fatiguing.
   Most video platforms show a square of what you look like on camera during a chat. But that's unnatural, Bailenson said. "In the real world, if somebody was following you around with a mirror constantly—so that while you were talking to people, making decisions, giving feedback, getting feedback—you were seeing yourself in a mirror, that would just be crazy. No one would ever consider that," he added.

   Solution: Bailenson recommends that platforms change the default practice of beaming the video to both self and others when it only needs to be sent to others. In the meantime, as stated previously, users should use the *hide self-view* button, which one can access by right clicking their own photo, once they see their face is framed properly in the video. As noted earlier, be sure to click it back on every once in a while, to be sure you're not too close to the screen or haven't slumped down in your chair.

3. Video chats dramatically reduce our usual mobility.
   In-person and audio phone conversations allow humans to walk around and move. But with videoconferencing, most cameras have a set field of view, meaning a person has to generally stay in the same spot. Movement is limited in ways that are not natural. "There's a growing research now that says when people are moving, they're performing better cognitively," Bailenson said.

4. The cognitive load is much higher in video chats.

Bailenson notes that in regular face-to-face interaction, non-verbal communication is quite natural, and each of us naturally makes and interprets gestures and nonverbal cues subconsciously. But in video chats, we have to work harder to send and receive signals.

Solution: During long stretches of meetings, give yourself an audio only break. "This is not simply you turning off your camera to take a break from having to be nonverbally active, but also turning your body away from the screen," Bailenson said, "so that for a few minutes you are not smothered with gestures that are perceptually realistic but socially meaningless."

This article: www.networx.com/article/a-guide-to-bathroom-euphamisms opens the (restroom?) door to all of the expressions and gives guidance as to acceptability in the workplace. They favor restroom and powder room. We still like *bio break*.[†]

Summary

You can't beat face-to-face meetings for the best communication. However, the world we live in demands that we often work virtually, and so, consistently running good virtual meetings is a skill that needs to be developed. It requires being mindful of the dynamics before, during, and after the meeting that can make or break this critical first time together.

Zoom Fatigue Reference

How Virtual Meetings Can Curb Idea Generation. www.nature.com/articles/s41586-022-04643-y.

https://news.stanford.edu/2021/02/23/four-causes-zoom-fatigue-solutions/.

---

† This is one of those situations where culture comes into play. In the United States, we often say *bio break* as a euphemism for using a bathroom, restroom, W.C., powder room, or loo.

CHAPTER 10

Case Study for Multiday Planning Meeting—Building a House

We realize that the artifacts created in this book may seem a little abstract, so we created this case study, which we'll use for the multiday planning chapter to bring the concepts closer to reality. Rich has co-written a book called *Green Project Management*, so we thought it would be interesting if we gave you an example that relates to a project focused on sustainability.

Our story features fictitious Mayor Karyn Salas of Escondido, California, a real city of about 150,000 people about 30 miles north of San Diego, with a median age of 33 years. With the passage of the *Global Warming Solutions Act of 2006* (a real thing—see our references.) California has become a world leader in progressive legislation aimed at curbing climate change. Considered to be one of the most successful pieces of environmental legislation, the bill required California to roll back its greenhouse gas emissions to 1990 levels by the year 2020, and it provided a framework for achieving that goal in a quantifiable and cost-effective way while boosting economic growth through green job creation.

In our story, Mayor Salas is nearing the end of her first term and is seeking re-election in an area where ecological concerns are front and center in the young electorate. Her platform calls for further buy-in to the *Go Green Escondido* program, started by her staff near the end of her first year in office. Ms. Salas has been an advocate of sustainable building, and she wants to demonstrate her commitment by building her own new home using the techniques she's been promoting.

She referred to *Green Principles for Residential Design* (Sustainable Buildings Industry Council 2016) for ideas and decided to implement several of these green building ideas into her own home—very publicly.

After all, what's a project but a conversion of ideas into reality? In particular, she's decided to focus on making these three ideas into reality:

- Minimizing energy use and using renewable energy strategies. This principle covers aspects such as the importance of dramatically reducing the overall energy loads (through insulation, efficient equipment and lighting, and careful detailing of the entire enclosure), limiting the amount of fossil fuels required, incorporating renewable energy systems such as photovoltaics, geothermal heat pumps, and solar water heating whenever feasible, and purchasing green power in order to minimize the creation of greenhouse gasses.
- Conserving and protecting water. This principle covers aspects such as reducing, controlling, or treating site runoff; designing and constructing the home to conserve water used inside and outside; and minimizing leaks by ensuring proper inspections during construction.
- Using environmentally preferable products. This principle covers such aspects as specifying products that are salvaged, are made with recycled content, are easily disassembled for reuse or recycling, conserve natural resources, reduce overall material use, are exceptionally durable or low maintenance, are naturally or minimally processed, save energy and/or water, and/or reduce pollution or waste from operations.

From these principles, she has chosen to integrate three related elements into her home construction project, with the thinking that they should be accessible technologies that others could readily implement, rather than over-reaching and building a wind farm or seeking Leadership in Energy and Environmental Design (LEED) platinum qualification for her house. Those elements include:

- Installing a Tesla solar roof
- Installing a rainwater capture system for nonpotable use (such as irrigation)
- Installing a hot tub

- Selecting and installing super high-efficiency heating and cooling systems
- Selecting a maximum of recycled and salvaged materials as described earlier, adding a step to the purchasing process in which she and a team of college interns from nearby Cal State University, San Marcos, oversee the selection of materials.

Now that you have the background of this case study, you'll better understand how it relates to productive planning meetings when you read the following chapter.

Reference

California Global Warming Solutions Act: https://ww2.arb.ca.gov/resources/fact-sheets/ab-32-global-warming-solutions-act-2006.

CHAPTER 11

Considerations for a Multiday Project Planning Meeting

Key Takeaways

- 🗨 The multiday meeting should be very carefully planned, just like a project, with its inherent risks.
- 🗨 If you don't know how to facilitate such a meeting, outsource it.
- 🗨 Have an agenda, but don't be afraid to modify it if circumstances dictate.
- 🗨 Be sure you know exactly what your objectives and deliverables are.
- 🗨 Communicate early and often.

Planning the Project Planning Meeting

Generally speaking, the type of multiday planning meeting we are going to describe initially is more commonly used in a waterfall project. So, the artifacts will be limited to that methodology, which, for all you may hear about Agile, is still the most commonly used project management methodology. Later in the chapter, we'll get to the closest analog we can think of in the Agile world, the two-day Program Increment meeting associated with the Scaled Agile Framework (SAFe®) methodology. (Note: multiday planning meetings tend to be two-day sessions, so we'll assume that for the sake of this discussion.)

One way or the other, any project planning meeting is going to cost you time and money to host. So, you want to be absolutely, positively, 100 percent ready to have, not a good but a *great* meeting and get a maximal return on your investment. People hate to go to one-hour meetings and have their time wasted. Imagine if they fly in from around the world or commit to multiple Zoom meetings only to find that you don't have your act together. *This is the person*, they will ask themselves, perhaps even in italics with a cartoon bubble over their head, *who is going to run our project?*

So, you must take time out of your busy schedule and plan for this session thoroughly. It will pay off. Start by asking yourself (and answering) some key questions:

- Who's facilitating the meeting? As project manager, are *you* running it? If so, do *you* have the facilitation (not to mention people) skills necessary to undertake such an endeavor?

- Who's attending the meeting? For our house-building project, we'll want the plumber, the electrician, the architect, the HVAC people, and so on. And, of course, be sure to invite the sponsor (who should have been in on all the planning anyway). Get the right people in the right room so that the right discussions can be had, and the right decisions made, with all the pertinent facts (not guesses or assumptions)! The converse is also true: if you leave someone out, you may hear them utter the dreaded phrase, "I wish you had asked *me*. I would have told you that you had to get an XYZ Permit before you could dig those trenches. Harrumph! I said *good day!*"

- Do you have an agenda? Have we hammered this home enough? Be sure you have an agenda, and that you've published it in advance. On the one hand, this agenda must be airtight so that everyone knows what's happening and when.
  Recalling our section *Be Sensory*, and using our case study example, our Mayor, Karyn, may well want to have a large artist's conception drawing of her home up on the wall for

everyone to see while the meeting goes on. Not only will it be a way to point out specific elements ("it turns out that the roof is the part here on the top"), but it will also serve as a reminder of the end product of the project. A not-so-subtle additional visual could be a *Salas 2020* campaign banner.

It all starts, however, with a good agenda. Following is an example (Figures 11.1a, 1b and 1c).

Sample Agenda

Meeting Objectives
- Gain full team understanding of the project
- Create the initial project schedule
- Create the initial list of risks along with risk response plans
- Validate the initial schedule and risk plan with the team
- Surface (and resolve) any resourcing issues

Meeting Outcomes
- A project with a significantly improved chance of success, due to a thoughtful and far-reaching plan
- Understanding of each team's perspective, roles, and responsibilities and a shared vision for the project's deliverables
- Buy-in from all key stakeholders

Meeting Deliverables
- A work breakdown structure (WBS) for each function
- Initial (draft) project schedule
- Initial list of project risks and issues
- Expanded list of stakeholders
- RACI– detail level will depend on available time

Prework (to be completed before the meeting)
- Provide detailed estimates as per attached guidelines
- Contributing functional groups (e.g., engineering, marketing, development) provide their individual functional strategies
- Review project documentation sent to you:
    - Current integrated schedule
    - Product definition document
- Assure that your current project documentation and strategy presentations are ready

Dress
- Business casual (working meeting)

Figure 11.1a Sample meeting agenda, page 1 of 3

Preliminary Timing (specific times may change slightly)

Day 1

8:30	**Opening**
	Welcome & purpose/expectations of the meeting
8:40	Functional strategy/management direction
	• Update from sponsor (10 min.)
	• Success criteria
	• Updates from functions (20 min.)
10:00	**Break**
10:15	Establish each function's work breakdown schedule
11:00	Finalization of integrated schedule
	• validation of key tasks
	• interdependencies
	• milestones
	• validation of timeline based on duration estimate
12:00	**Lunch** (ordered-in based on your logged preferences)
12:45	Continue with integrated schedule work
14:00	**Break**
14:15	Continue with integrated schedule work
17:00	Review and summary
17:30	**Close**

Figure 11.1b Sample meeting agenda, Page 2 of 3

Day 2

8:30	Review of prior days' work (30 minutes)
	Review of draft schedule
9:00	Schedule compression (2 hours)
	• revisiting dependency assumptions
	• crashing (adding resources)
	• fast tracking (parallel tasks)
10:00	**Break**
10:15	Continue with Schedule compression
11:00	Risk Identification Planning
	• validate previously identified risks
	• prioritize risks
	• identify risk triggers
12:00	**Lunch** (in work groups, as indicated)

Figure 11.1c (Continues)

12:45	Risk response planning
14:45	**Break**
15:00	Key messages
16:00	Next steps and action summary
16:30	**Close**

12:45 Risk response planning
- decide how to respond critical risks
- monitor other risks

15:00 Key messages
- issues that require highest attention from management

Figure 11.1c Sample meeting agenda, Page 3 of 3

Meeting Agenda Tips

- **Emphasize that the meeting will start on time.** Pragmatically, you may choose to give a five- or 10-minute grace period for traffic issues, dropping kids at school, and that's fine. Have a conference bridge set up. Latecomers who are stuck in traffic can dial in and attend virtually until they arrive.
- **Have a risk response plan** for this two-day project. What if there's a power failure? Or an emergency? Or an unexpected weather condition? Have a Plan B in your pocket.
- **Plan for two full days**, from 8 a.m. to 5:30 p.m. If you publish an agenda that shows the meeting adjourning at 3:30 on Day 2, everyone will set their watch (and make travel arrangements) based on that.
- **Ask attendees to give this matter their full attention.** Everyone will have other meetings they should be attending. As much as possible, ask them not to schedule any during this time.
- **Set expectations.** Your attendees are, for all intents and purposes, your stakeholders. See Figure 11.2 to understand that stakeholders will have varying levels of attitude, power, and interest. For example, a *Tripwire* is a stakeholder with a potentially negative attitude, who isn't currently powerful or interested, but should they gain power and/or get interested, they could become a problem (an *Irritant* or *Saboteur* in the chart). In any case, know your stakeholders, and engage them. You want there to be no doubt as to why you're convening. The last thing you need is people showing up and saying, "I thought we were going to discuss the color of the house." No,

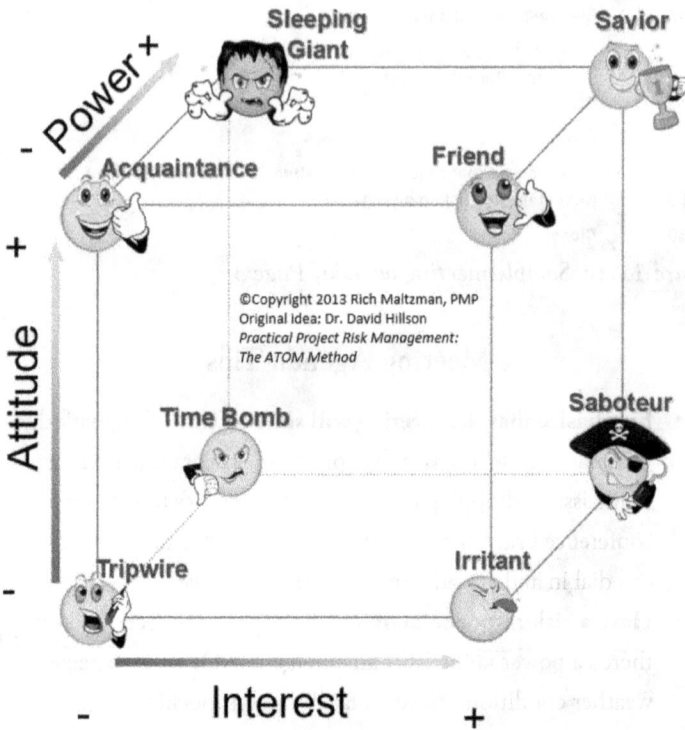

Figure 11.2 *Know your stakeholder types in three dimensions*

that's a requirement and should have already been determined. You're there for specific reasons, and they shouldn't be a secret.

- **Address *hidden agendas*** (ulterior motives). Not everyone on your project team is necessarily as enthusiastic about your project as you are. They may even be (see Figure 11.2) a Saboteur! If you know that, say, Marco over in operations finds your project to be a threat to him, best to know that now and address it with the sponsor. The sponsor may know that already. The sponsor needs (or you both need) to have a conversation with Bob and perhaps with his boss.

- **Hold a preliminary phone call** (or two). Let people ask questions. Ask what they'd want to get out of such a meeting (as presenters and as attendees). Listen intently to their concerns. They're much easier to correct at the premeeting stage than in the middle of the meeting, or worse, during the execution of the project!

- **Decide who will be the scribe for the meeting**. Every single word that's spoken doesn't have to be written down. But someone will need to summarize the meeting and notate outcomes, actions taken, actions assigned, and so on.
- **Assign prework**, as necessary. Some, and possibly all teams may want to do a presentation. Sometimes, if it's a technical solution you're working on, a team member may have to bring a prototype. Be sure that everyone understands their prework and follow up with them as needed to ensure that they're prepared.
- **You—yes, you!—may also have some prework to do**. On at least one of our engagements, the customer wanted to precreate the work breakdown structures in order to save time in the session. We also suggest starting an initial list of risks. There are *always* risks (not enough resources, time, budget), so it's best to put those on the table right away.
- **Stay as focused on possible on the most important artifacts**. As your goal is to produce certain artifacts in a very limited amount of time, stay laser-focused on that list.
- **Be sure you have all the project prerequisites.** In order to do the work of this planning session, you must have certain information. For example, requirements for the product or service should be fairly well-understood. In our house-building case, we need to know that the house is a ranch that will have, say, three bedrooms, an indoor pool, and a two-car garage.
- **Create a RACI matrix.** This is one form of a responsibility assignment matrix, and it maps the what (the tasks of the project) to the who (the contributors to the project). *RACI* stands for responsible, accountable, consulted, and informed (see Figure 11.3), and at the intersection of the what and the who, defines just what the contributor contributes. There is an RACI template for your use on our our website. That conflict (well-managed) can be a source of creative problem-solving. So, be prepared for disagreements and some conflict, which can be on several levels of 'maturity', as described in Graham's hierarchy of disagreement (see Figure 11.4). The low levels of this hierarchy are not productive. As a great facilitator, you can be the one to elevate the conversation.

This is a partial listing of what might be in a RACI (reduced for size purposes)

House Building Project	Architect	Plumber	Electrician	Environmental SME	Publicist	PROJECT MGR
Identify a minimum of three contractors from Angie's List	R	-	-	-	-	I
Arrange contractor visits and quotations	A	-	-	-	-	R
Ensure all wiring is complete	C	I	A	-	-	I
Ensure that all components comply with LEED specs	I	I	-	A/R	I	I
Coordinate communications among all stakeholders	-	-	-	-	-	A/R
Ensure that all plumbing is complete	I	A	I	I	-	I
Investigate best solution for implementing cistern	C	C	I	A	-	C
Coordinate communications with press and campaign	C	-	-	C	A	C

Figure 11.3 An RACI matrix from our case study

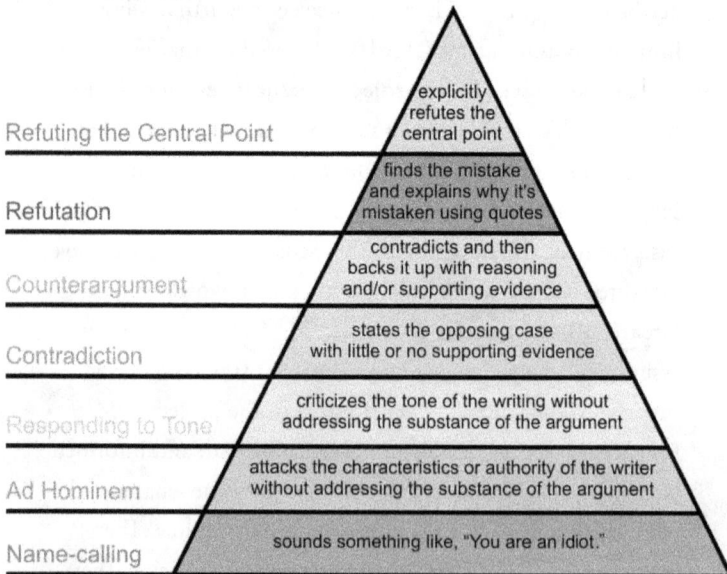

Refuting the Central Point	explicitly refutes the central point
Refutation	finds the mistake and explains why it's mistaken using quotes
Counterargument	contradicts and then backs it up with reasoning and/or supporting evidence
Contradiction	states the opposing case with little or no supporting evidence
Responding to Tone	criticizes the tone of the writing without addressing the substance of the argument
Ad Hominem	attacks the characteristics or authority of the writer without addressing the substance of the argument
Name-calling	sounds something like, "You are an idiot."

Figure 11.4 Graham's hierarchy of disagreement

By *Loudacris*. Modified by Rocket000 [CC BY 3.0 (https://creativecommons.org/licenses/by/3.0)], via Wikimedia Commons.

War Story—An Animal Approach to Conflict

We walked into the meeting a couple of minutes late. My mentor, Pete, a California native who grew up surfing, was calm and almost laid back as he took a seat. I, on the other hand, was ready to throw up in the garbage can near the door. Pete had 15 years of project management experience. I had two weeks. We were coming into a meeting where conflict was inevitable. On each side of the square table sat four members of different product teams. One was for online content and the other print publication. The *new school* didn't like the *old school*.

Pete took a breath and started the meeting. Immediately there was yelling, finger pointing, swearing, blaming, and more yelling. I tried to remain calm, but I'm pretty sure I was sweating. Pete leaned back and watched. After a good minute or two of this, I leaned forward to say something when Pete grabbed my arm and whispered "Let the animals kill each other. Make friends with the survivors." I didn't know what he meant right away, but after a few more minutes, the yelling and arguing among all but two people stopped.

Pete took a few notes, and during a lull in the conversation, spoke up. He pointed out all the similarities in the discussion and noted the differences weren't that big. Eventually they reached an agreement, but Pete took some lashings too. As uncomfortable as that was, it was a lesson to not avoid conflict and to sometimes let it play out.

—Jason Orloske, via LinkedIn

- Be sure all your technology works in advance. Ensure that your Wi-Fi works, and that everyone has the password. Put it on a flip chart; otherwise, people will forget and ask you every five minutes to remind them what it is.

- Decide where to hold the meeting. In a perfect world, we suggest holding it off-site at a nearby hotel conference room. This gets everyone away from their work environment and allows them to focus.
- Be sure you have the right materials. You'll need the following: flip charts, markers, sticky notes, adhesive tape, name tags, wireless access, power strips, notepads and pens, and a spare laptop.
- Have the support you'll need. Be sure your administrative assistant is on top of things and can run out and get anything you need. If you're holding the meeting internally, have phone numbers for IT support.
- Set a dress code. It should mirror your company's culture, but be sure people are dressed comfortably but not sloppily. And suggest that people bring a light sweater, no matter what the time of year.
- Check the room setup. You might want to set up the room initially as a large roundtable, or long tables in a U-shape, and later break it down into pods, or teams, working together. Think this through in advance. No surprises! Again, you don't want to spend time deciding on these things during the meeting. The bottom line: do not be surprised by your room! Hotels host meetings routinely, and they can provide you with just about any room configuration you would like.
- Set up a document repository. If you're using a repository tool such as SharePoint, be sure it's set up premeeting. Upload all the artifacts you'll be using in the meeting and be sure the team knows it's there and how to use it. Everyone should be able to access it inside and outside of firewalls. This can be established as an ongoing virtual location for knowledge sharing and collaboration throughout the project.
- Publish a roster. It should include names, roles, and contract information for each team member. Be sure it's

in your repository. This will become an important project artifact.

- Create and circulate a communications plan. Using the template from our website, http://projectmeetings.us, show the team how communications will flow. For example, there might be a weekly team meeting to discuss action items, schedule, and risks. There might be a monthly steering committee meeting to advise senior management of progress. There might be a lessons learned meeting at the end of each phase to determine what can be done better.

- Expect resistance. The team needs to understand what a facilitator's role is (one of us worked on a project where the group even questioned the *need* for a facilitator). *The meeting does not run itself.* As we said earlier, don't assume that everyone knows what you know. Your attendees have a million other things to do, so take that into consideration.

- Plan a fun activity for the evenings. It could be attending, or even participating in, a sporting event or a dinner. Socializing gives team members a chance to get to know each other better outside of the work environment. This is when the pictures of the kids, dogs, iguanas, yetis, and cats come out, which is all to the group's benefit—consider it an important part of the forming stage of team building.

  o Cautionary tale on this. A colleague of ours told us that one guy in her group had a little too much to drink and "said something to a female team member that couldn't be unsaid." Watch alcohol intake.

- Pay attention to logistics, directions, and security. We've lost track of the number of times we've been invited to a meeting and been given simple directions, only to discover that "137 Main Street" represented a complex of 12 business condominiums. And once we found the building, we discovered that no one at the front desk knew who we were, *and* we had to go through security, get a badge, and watch a video. You want to avoid this situation at all costs. The last thing you need at a meeting is people showing up an hour late, angry because they had no idea how to find the building, never mind the conference room. Be sure they all have your mobile number and check it frequently. Remember that some people are risk-seeking when it comes to scheduling and will leave for your meeting roughly around the time it's supposed to start.

- Use a planning meeting readiness checklist. It will help ensure that you don't miss a step. The sponsor should review the checklist and sign off on it. "Dude," your attendees will say admiringly, "you thought of everything."

Planning Meeting Readiness Checklist

- ❑ Facilitator and, if need be, co-facilitator chosen
- ❑ Attendee list decided on and reviewed by sponsor
- ❑ Agenda created and published
- ❑ Preliminary phone call(s) done
- ❑ Facilitator pre-work completed
- ❑ Project or product requirements understood
- ❑ Project charter and scope statement created
- ❑ Pre-work assigned
- ❑ Initial list of risks created
- ❑ Initial Assumption Log created
- ❑ Relevant information from previous projects
- ❑ Front desk and security logistics complete and communicated
- ❑ Room Logistics verified
- ❑ Preliminary work assigned
- ❑ SharePoint or other common area available for document sharing

Figure 11.5 Planning meeting checklist

War Story—Requirements

In our project, we had a business analyst (BA) who was very focused and deliberate—so we got very well-defined requirements, but she took forever to get them to us. We were faced with a deadline to get final approval on a set of requirements finalized by the end of this meeting. In fact, the BA was to go on vacation immediately following the meeting and would be unreachable—so this was a true hard cutoff.

So, our objective for this one hour meeting I was facilitating was very clear. Finalize the requirements (there were three of them) and get them to the vendor to trigger the next activity.

About 15 minutes into the meeting—out of nowhere—another requirement came up. Typically, a new requirement like this, all by itself, have taken an hour or more to resolve. So, we now had 45 minutes in which to do 70- or 80-minutes' worth of work.

As the PM and facilitator, I had the choice to try to defer this requirement (that just would not have worked with this group), or I could adapt to the new conditions. I decided to let this play out—to minimally facilitate, but to also watch the time and when necessary, make the team aware of our time constraints—all the while acknowledging their progress.

This turned out to be the best decision I could have made as a facilitator. In about 30 minutes, the team reviewed, resolved, and approved the new requirement and then jumped on the scheduled original requirements. This affirms two ideas about meetings: (1) although it's a great idea to have an agenda, you need to be ready to tear it up mid-meeting and facilitate on the fly and (2) sometimes deferring to the cadence and process of the business group is the best decision.

—Anonymous at author's request

Sponsor

After everyone arrives and is settled, well-fed, and set up, the sponsor should speak to the group. As discussed in the planning session, she now has a group in front of her and can deliver a message that helps attendees understand the rationale and importance of the project in a larger context. Although this sponsor message is time taken away from the specifics of the project and the creation of artifacts, the motivation and alignment it provides (if done well) will more than make up for that.

The sponsor's goal is to accomplish several things:

- State, or restate, the purpose of this session. People want to know (and deserve to know) why you need two days of their time. You may have already said this prior to the meeting. But let's remind you of this adage (often attributed to Aristotle who reportedly used it in his sales meetings):
  - Tell them what you're going to tell them.
  - Tell them.
  - Tell them what you told them.
- Provide an overview of the project. Sponsors are invariably at a senior level, so they typically have a better picture of how the project fits into the organization. What priority does it have? How does executive management see it? People like to be on projects that are not only interesting to work on but that have some import to the company.
- Introduce the facilitator. If the sponsor and/or project manager are facilitating, this step will be unnecessary. If you've hired a facilitator, the team needs to know exactly what his or her role is. And they need to know that they have your, and the facilitator's, full faith, confidence, and respect. Effectively, the facilitator's job is to move the meeting along and keep it on track.
- Establish and enforce ground rules. It's easy for some people to dominate a conversation and perhaps intimidate others. (See goblins.) This must not happen, and it's the job of the facilitator to prevent it, with the enforcement of the sponsor if possible.
- Answer questions. No matter how well you prepare, people will have questions. The sponsor should endeavor to answer them as honestly as possible. Often the question will involve

resources. How, they will ask, can they accomplish this project as well as all the other ones they're working on?

- Explain the process. Many team members have never attended a session such as this. The sponsor should explain that the meeting and the artifacts it creates are part of a time-honored project management technique, and that it was decided to incorporate them as a gesture toward best practices.
- Review the critical success factors. What elements need to be in place for the team to succeed? These elements might include quick access to the sponsor to resolve issues, a good communications plan, sufficient budget, and so on. Critical success factors are different from success criteria, or objectives, which are things such as *delivered on-time, delivered on-budget*, and *captured X percent of market*. See our table in the Glossary.

Project Manager and Sponsor

Now that the groundwork has been set by the sponsor, it's incumbent upon the project manager to explain how the project will be run and what tools will be used. Take the time to explain this—in many organizations, best practices are not used to their full extent. Explain that you're doing this in order to have better control of the project so that it meets its objectives.

Artifacts you will most likely create:

- Schedule. Whether you use Microsoft Project, Primavera, Excel, Smartsheet, or some enterprisewide project management software, it's greatly advantageous to show the team what the schedule will look like when complete (begin with the end in mind). This is *not* training for the tool, just a way for them to see how the pieces all interact. Make sure you have a summary task view and/or a milestone chart.
- Risk register. The sponsor (and possibly functional managers) should have been able to identify a list of preliminary risks. Display this and discuss how risk management will be an

important part of your process going forward. Also explain that the team will be learning how to do risk analysis during this meeting, and that they will be developing a list of risks along with possible responses to those risks.

Functional Presentations

Each contributing function (in our case study, these would be architects, electricians, plumbers, and roofers) should be encouraged to provide a presentation on the project from their viewpoint. This presentation should be brief, but it needs to be to-the-point and effective.

In our sample agenda, we set aside an hour for functional strategy/ management direction (see Figure 11.5). It could be more or less time, depending on how many functions there are and how involved the technical details are. But it's up to the facilitator to be sure that things move along. And, of course, impromptu breakout sessions will occur. Let them. Breakout sessions should be encouraged, but not at the expense of the group working together on artifacts.

Assumptions

In order to proceed with any sort of project work, we must list our assumptions. These assumptions can grow or shrink over the course of the project, and they're the precursors of risk. How many projects have failed because the team didn't consciously record and communicate their working assumptions? Our opinion, based on experience of many decades, is that this rate is over 50 percent. For example, if you're working on an international project and you make the assumption that the exchange rate between the involved countries is stable, there's a built-in threat that this exchange rate will change and cause issues with resources coming from a formerly low-cost country.

Assumptions in our sample case might be:

- The architect will be available 40 hours a week during the planning phase.
- The highest-quality building materials will be used.
- The project manager will work on no more than one project in addition to this one.

Are these all true facts? No. They have not yet happened! They are assumptions, statements that we are asserting to be true for planning purposes. If they are not true, they become threats.

Constraints

Constraints are different from assumptions but are often mentioned in the same breath. Let's take a look at our Glossary definition: "A limiting factor that affects the execution of a project."

Why would we have constraints? They are a fact of life of any project. Perhaps in the days of building the pyramids, we had none. But in modern project management, we have many limiting factors. For example:

- Budget (cost). If your budget for this project is $10M, then it can't simultaneously be $11M.
- Schedule. If the house is scheduled to be completed by August 31, then that is a limiting factor against which you must work.
- Scope. You're not building a 20-room mansion; you're building a three-bedroom house.

In fact, those three items are classically called the triple constraint or the iron triangle. And in the best projects, these items—for every project—are ranked. So, you might ask the sponsor which of these three is most important. If she says, for example, scope first, budget second, schedule third, then you have your marching orders.

Figure 11.6 shows an example from our case study in which we could use a constraint priority matrix to determine the ruling constraint.

There will be other, project-specific constraints as well, such as (in our house example) being unable to build on certain areas due to the environmental regulations, or a constraint based on the fact that many

	Enhance: Top Priority	Constrain: Middle Priority	Accept: Lowest Priority	Comments
Schedule		◆◆		A late project will not reflect well, so this is imporant but less so than budget.
Cost	◆◆◆			Given that Karyn will be judged on how she manages a budget, this is tops.
Scope			◆	If a feature or two must be sacrificed, that's not good, but something's got to give.

Figure 11.6 Know thy constraint priorities!

of your construction crew are members of a religious group that forbids work on every other Wednesday afternoon in May, between noon and midnight. And in the Middle the workweek is Sunday through Thursday.

Estimating

Estimating is a task that everyone has to do, and no one loves. That's because people are never really sure how long something will take. Five days? Ten days? In addition, they don't want to commit. If they tell you that an activity will take 10 days and it actually takes 15, not only do they feel that they have let you down, but they also feel that they're causing the project to be late.

Please note the connection between estimation and risk. We like to say that each estimate is an example of risk, by definition. Five days may be three (an opportunity) or 12 (a threat). Each task length, or budget estimate, is only a single point from a future that we don't yet know. So, estimation and risk are inexorably intertwined.

The Work Breakdown Structure

As mentioned in the Glossary, the work breakdown structure (WBS) is a deliverable-oriented, detailed breakdown that defines the work packages and tasks at a level above that defined in the networks and schedules. This is a fundamental underpinning of project management planning that goes all the way back to the U.S. Department of Defense in the 1950s. To this day, the U.S. government still uses WBSs for all their projects, as do their government contractors.

The purpose of a WBS is to outline and visibly diagram the *what* of the work—in particular, what's in, and, by its absence, what's out. Think of it as a hierarchical map of the project's scope. Each function will have a WBS, and it should detail what work needs to be done by each function. It's very important to note, and for you to instruct, that the WBS is none of these:

- A timeline
- A bill of materials

- A budget
- A schedule
- A list of resources, or assignments to tasks

The WBS is the enabler of all those things, but it's *not* those things. It's important that the planning team, with you as the facilitator, focus the team on only the *what*, and avoid getting hung up on duration, dependencies, assignments, costs ... yet. When the WBS is complete, the team should be able to stand back and say, "*That's* what we need to do to complete our part of the project." That said, know this—the team will not instantly agree on how the WBS should be done or even exactly what's on it. That's okay! That's to be expected and is, in fact, part of the process.

Schedule

If all goes well, the teams should be ready to develop the schedule shortly after discussing the WBS. Before you begin, it would be well to be sure the team understands the difference between a plan and a schedule, as many people have a tendency to conflate their meanings. (Note: If some teams are still working on their own WBSs, it's perfectly okay to start capturing information in the schedule. Overlap is acceptable.)

The reason for having a good schedule, in part, is that you can, and should, link all the project activities in a dynamic view. In this way, if an activity slips, you can note that slippage in the schedule, and it will push out dates accordingly. There's no such facility for this in Excel.

Advise your teams that your goal for the session is to have a schedule displaying dependencies, dates, and milestones. Advise them further that you don't expect to have a finalized schedule by the end of two days, but rather a good first pass at a schedule. And that the work they did in creating the WBS will inform the schedule.

Risk Analysis and Identification

To recap, by now, you've created your functional WBSs, and you have a good initial draft schedule. It's time now to figure out what your risks are. As per the Glossary, *risk* is defined as "an uncertain event, which, if it occurs, has a positive or negative effect on one or more project objectives." A risk is something that *may* happen, not something that *will* happen. The latter is a fact—perhaps an issue or a risk that *has* happened. If Jane is going on maternity leave, that's a fact. Her absence, however, has triggered a risk to your project's objectives, which means that you'll either have to postpone the project or find another resource.

So, it's important to determine what the threats are to your project, and it's also important to identify the possible things that could go horribly right. (We call those opportunities.) The good news is that we now have an excellent idea of what our activities are, and with those and the WBS, we can now start to look at risks. In fact, you may well have put some risks on your parking lot flip chart while you were doing your previous work.

Once your risks are identified, they go into an ever evolving and constantly updated risk register. In the register, the risks are clearly explained, including what their impact will be on the project, and a first pass at a risk response.

But how do we get to that end result? Well, as risk is measured in terms of probability and impact, the first thing you'll want to do is create what we call a probability and impact matrix (some call it a heat map) on a flip chart on the wall as shown in Figure 11.7.

A heat map is simply a form of probability and impact (or PI) matrix that has been colorized so that the northeast corner is red, and the southwest corner is green, with commensurate shading of yellows in between to indicate that high combinations of probability and impact (for threats) are worthy of escalation (they're red) and threats that have combinations of low impact and/or low probability don't need as much attention (they're green). Following is a P/I matrix template. Next to that is an example of a heat map from our house-building case study.

You can see that the goal is to take every single risk identified and decide on its probability of occurring and its impact if it does. Is there a certain amount of subjectivity to this? Sure. But if your team has been doing this kind of work for a while, they should know the risks. And clearly, the ones in the upper-right quadrant will be of much greater concern than those in the lower left.

Once the matrix is done, the team should, literally, stand back and look at it. The P/I matrix should show every risk they can think of, with probabilities and impacts. (Okay, you have to draw the line somewhere.

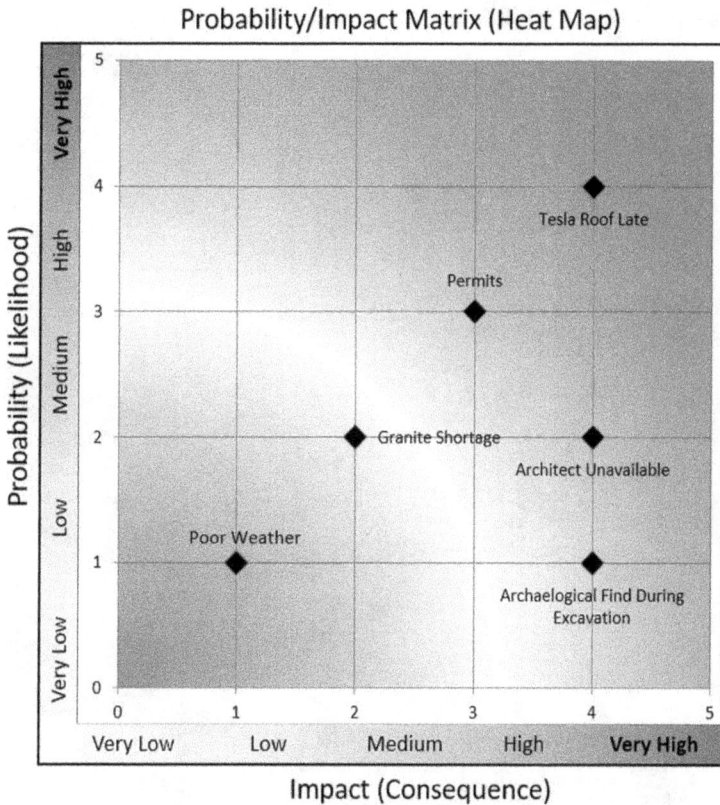

Figure 11.7 Case study probability/impact matrix

An asteroid hitting a manufacturing plant is a possibility, but unless you see that as a real threat, keep it [and those types of unlikely risks] off your matrix. On the other hand, the possibility of a hurricane in Florida, or a nor'easter in New England, is very real.)

There are certainly risks no one can see coming. We call these unknown unknowns. COVID-19 was such a beast. And of course (as our Monty Python fans know), no one *expects* the Spanish Inquisition.

Now that you've generated your list of prioritized risks, the next step is to put them into a ranked risk register. There's no particular tool that must be used to store your list of risks, but spreadsheets lend themselves quite well to this. Our template can assist you.

What you'll want to do is simple—put the risks in the register in ranked order based on your P/I results. When it's done, it should look something like what's shown in Figure 11.8.

ID	Threat /Oppty	Date raised	Risk Category	Risk Triggers (things th	Risk description	Prob	Impact	Severity (P * I)	Owner	Our team's response	Secondary Risks	Residual Risk	Status	Comments
T1	Threat	9/4/2022	Subcontractors	Reports just in from other customers of Myerson Framers indicate poor performance	If Framing Contractor fails to perform, all of the many dependent tasks that follow may slip commensurately, causing the project to be late.	4	5	20 - RED	Jen Tolm	Have subcontractor Billingsley Framers available on a standby basis.	We have to pay a "holding fee" of $1500 to Billingsley Framers.	Billingsley may also fail to perform.	Open, pending decision to purchase "holding fee"	
O1	Oppty	8/6/2022	Labor	News indicates that students from eastern Europe are flocking to our area for summer work (at low wages)	If summer workers become available, we could hire them, saving construction costs by 20%.	3	3	9 - YELLOW	Kim Yu	Advertise on Facebook and Instagram sites viewed by these students	These workers may not perform as expected. Fees for advertisement add to budget.	No response to advertisements	Open, pending decision to advertise	

Figure 11.8 Risk register snippet

Risk Response

The question now becomes what to *do* about those risks. Certainly, you'll want to focus heavily on the ones at the top of your ranking, and perhaps some of the medium-level ones. (The Project Management Institute suggests that you put the lower-ranked ones on a watchlist because those can easily bubble up if left unwatched and become major risks.)

For threats, we can respond in the following five ways:

- Escalate. This response is for those threats that are outside the scope of the project or that require greater authority than that granted to the project manager.
- Accept. Let it happen, either without doing anything (passive acceptance) or with some form of contingency plan (active acceptance).
- Mitigate. Try to change the probability of the threat and/or the impact of the threat if it does occur.
- Avoid. Change the plan to not even deal with that threat. Normally when we avoid, we're also avoiding some benefit.
- Transfer. Give the threat to someone else—usually for a large fee.

Note that there are also positive project risks—opportunities, which have equal and opposite responses like the aforementioned (Hillson 2001): exploit, enhance, share, ignore. It is also a good idea to consider *overall* project risks, those that are overarching and, in a way, trivialize the other threats.

Think of overall project risk as those risks that overarch the entire project. If, for example, your project is to ship a delicate package on a large seagoing vessel to another continent, you would identify risks such as poor packaging of the item in a box, careful transport of the box from your location to the ship's dock, and so on. However, if your box is being shipped via the HMS *Titanic*, there's an overall project threat, called *The Titanic Sinks*. This is represented very well in a one-minute video that you can find at bit.ly/titanicsinks. In our case study, an earthquake in Karyn's worksite area would be an example.

Once you've broadly and deeply identified risks, you'll collaborate with your team to brainstorm the proper type of response, and the specific action to implement that response, for each risk in the risk register.

Agile and Large Project Planning

The Agile Manifesto and framework do a very good job in describing life on a project for a single team. But as we've seen in our discussion on project planning, often there are multiple cross-functional teams involved in a project. For this, the Scaled Agile Framework (SAFe®) (among others) was developed. We'll focus on SAFe® as it's the most popular and one of us is certified in it.

SAFe® promotes alignment, collaboration, and delivery across large numbers of Agile teams. It was developed, by and for practitioners, by leveraging three primary bodies of knowledge: Agile software development, lean product development, and systems thinking.

How Does SAFe® Differ From Nonscaled Agile?

SAFe® introduces a concept called the Agile release train (ART). This is defined as

> a long-lived team of Agile teams, which, along with other stakeholders, develops and delivers solutions incrementally, using a series of fixed-length iterations within a program increment (PI) timebox. The ART aligns teams to a common business and technology mission.

Program Increments

A program increment (PI) is a timebox during which an ART delivers incremental value in the form of working, tested software, and systems. PIs are typically 8 to 12 weeks long.

The most common pattern for a PI is four development iterations, followed by one innovation and planning (IP) iteration. It's a fixed timebox for building and validating a full system increment, demonstrating value, and getting fast feedback.

New Roles

There is a SAFe®-specific role called the release train engineer (RTE). The RTE is a servant leader and coach for the ART or team of teams. The RTE's major responsibilities are to facilitate the ART events and processes and assist the teams in delivering value. RTEs communicate with stakeholders, escalate impediments, help manage risk, and drive improvement.

SAFe® Planning Meetings

PI planning is a face-to-face event that aligns all the teams with a shared mission and vision. Distributed teams may use remote communication methods such as we have discussed in Chapter 10 in order to be part of the meeting. The planning meeting is typically two days long and is facilitated by the RTE, a coach of coaches who encourages cooperation. As in a large, more traditional, waterfall planning session, business context and vision are presented, followed by team planning breakouts. Essentially, each team is a Scrum team with its own Scrum master and product owner. The planning meeting occurs during the IP iteration.

PI Planning Deliverables

There are two SMART (specific, measurable, achievable, relevant, time-bound) objectives for each team aligned with business value, and a program board, which shows delivery dates, milestones, and dependencies among teams. Some will recognize the latter as a swimlane visual (Figure 11.9).

Meeting Activities

This meeting is very similar in some respects to a waterfall planning meeting. The business owner (sponsor) talks about how current customer business needs are being met. Product management talks about the product vision and milestones.

The RTE presents the planning process and expected outcomes of the meeting. Teams estimate their velocity for each iteration and identify

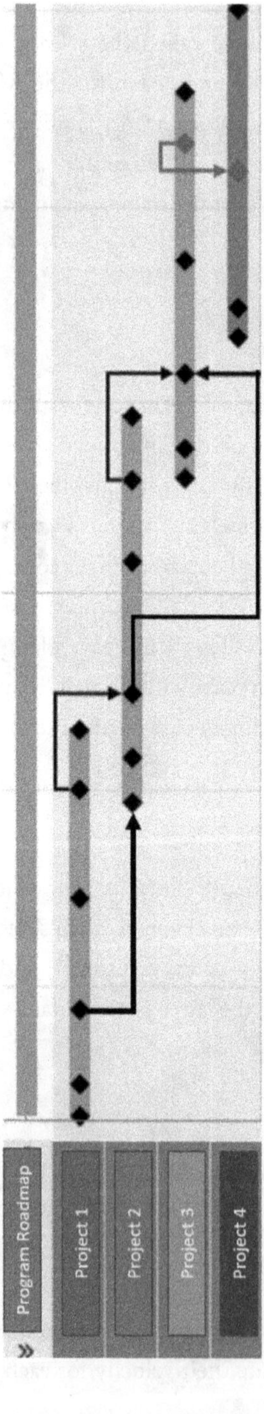

Figure 11.9 Program roadmap example

backlog items. They begin working on their team PI objectives. Features get added to the program board.

Teams present their plans, which get critiqued by other teams and management. The goal is to find scope issues, risks, or dependencies. The RTE keeps everyone on track and facilitates discussion. It's not his or her job to direct proceedings.

On the second day, any results and changes from the previous day are discussed. Teams continue planning, incorporating necessary adjustments. Objectives are finalized, and the business owners assign business value.

During the final plan review, all teams present plans to the group. Risks and impediments are identified. No attempt is made to remove impediments in this time frame, but mitigation plans are made for any program-level risks.

Management Acceptance of Commitments

One method Agilists use to gauge acceptance of a commitment is to execute the simple concept called *fist of five*, which is just holding up anywhere from one to five fingers to vote on something. Each team conducts a fist-of-five vote. If the average is three fingers or above, then management should accept the commitment. If it's less than three, the team reworks the plan.

Any items that don't have a vote of confidence might add to the list of risks or require replanning. Teams are given the opportunity to rework their plans until there's a high level of confidence.

Lastly, as in Scrum, the RTE leads a retrospective for the PI planning event to record what went well and what didn't.

On leaving the PI planning event, teams and product owners have not only a good sense of the roadmap but also a backlog for the upcoming PI. The RTE maintains a list of the risks.

It should be noted that there are a significant number of Agilists—and one of the authors' acquaintance—who feel that SAFe® is too process-bound, too command-and-control-oriented and not really Agile at all. Nevertheless, as noted, it is demonstrably the most popular scaled version of Agile. And it is the authors' contention that purity in and of itself is not the goal. *Results* are.*

So, you can see that the world of Agile is different—it has different working assumptions, different terminology, different ways of working. Still, many of the overall tips and guidance in this book will apply to project meetings of either an Agile or waterfall nature.

If you're seeking more information on how exactly to perform Scrum, you should certainly check out the Agile Manifesto along with its principles and the separate *Scrum Guide*.

- Agile 101, The Agile Alliance (www.agilealliance.org/agile101/)
- The Agile Manifesto (www.agilemanifesto.org)
- Scrum Alliance (www.scrumalliance.org)
- Scaled Agile Framework (www.scaledagileframework.com)
- *Scrum Guide* (www.scrum.org/resources/scrum-guide)

Summary

If a project is important enough and especially if it is crucial to the organization, it may be necessary to have a multiday planning meeting. But as this will take a lot of time for a potentially significant number of people, it is important to be sure that it is well planned, and that all who come to it have the same set of expectations.

Reference

Hillson, D. 2001. "Effective strategies for exploiting opportunities." www.pmi.org/learning/library/effective-strategies-exploiting-opportunities-7947.

---

* A very viable alternative to SAFe® is Scrum@Scale® which one of the authors is currently working with. It is much less process-bound, organic, and closer to the spirit of Agile. The authors chose not to use it as it has no two-day planning session.

CHAPTER 12

Adjournment

Thinking of a book as a meeting (which, in a way, it is, and by the way, nice meeting you!), we have reached the end of the meeting—adjournment. Now that you've read our book, perhaps you'll see there's more—a lot more—to meetings and meeting facilitation than meets the eye. However, no matter how much we may love meetings, well, nobody *else* does.

So, as we've related in the book, our job is to make our meetings stand out, make people *want* to come to our meetings because they get things done. Project meetings planned and run the right way get things done because we:

- Have a solid reason for meeting
- Invite the right people
- Have an agenda
- Work that agenda
- Read the room (and adapt to that reading)
- Control the discussion
- Don't allow the meeting to be hijacked
- Leave the room with action items
- Follow up (postmeeting)

At the end of the day, it's not meetings we're dealing with—it's people. Good old flesh and blood people, not robots. (Not yet anyway.) In fact, we would argue that the knowledge, skills, and abilities you have gained in reading this book will give you an advantage in a world that already has artificial intelligence (AI) making routine project jobs like planning and scheduling on the verge of obsolete (see the following box). The more interpersonal skills you develop (and facilitating project meetings is definitely one!), the better off you are from an employability standpoint. You have seen that understanding participants' motivations, engaging with stakeholders, and building communications skills are all part of planning and running a powerful, successful meeting.

Artificial Intelligence and Meetings

The release of ChatGPT (Chat Generative Pre-trained Transformer) in November 2022 was a game-changer. Certainly, artificial intelligence (AI) had been around for a while so that technology was no surprise.

What *was* a surprise to users was its overall conversational fluency. As noted on creator OpenAI's website, "we've trained a model called ChatGPT which interacts in a conversational way. The dialogue format makes it possible for ChatGPT to answer follow-up questions, admit its mistakes, challenge incorrect premises, and reject inappropriate requests."

A recent Goldman Sachs report says that AI systems like ChatGPT "could impact 300 million full-time jobs worldwide, with administrative and legal roles some of the most at risk."

For our purposes as project managers, AI tools might be able to assist us in some of the more mundane tasks of project management such as generating reports. In fact, why not ask an expert on this topic? So, we asked the current version of ChatGPT to tell us the effect of AI on project management jobs. Here is its response:

> AI is likely to have a significant impact on project management jobs, as it can automate routine tasks and provide valuable insights, allowing project managers to focus on more strategic work. However, it may also lead to the need for new skills and the potential for job displacement in certain areas.

More to the point of meetings, tools like, otter.ai might assist during Zoom or Teams meetings. It is a "meeting assistant that records audio, writes notes, automatically captures slides, and generates summaries." One of the authors has had the occasion to use it and it seems to capture data quite well.

One "gotcha" to watch out for with tools like this is that according to (at least) U.S. law, attendees at a meeting *must know they are being recorded* and should be advised there is a transcript being made. Laws vary state-by-state as to whether or not both sides should be advised. Tread with caution.

Note that when we say, "Read the room, or Read a person…," it's not for any malevolent purpose—it's done so that we can fully understand and decode the messages they're sending us whether verbal or otherwise. Many people are nonconfrontational, but one way or the other will find a way to communicate how they feel (sometimes with encouragement from you—their servant leader). And you need to have your antennae up to receive those subtle messages.

Now while yes, we talked about body language and the importance of planning and virtual meetings and all the great tools that go with those, we would like to remind you about something important and that is....

Humor. Yes, spelled with or without an extra *U*, we are talking about injecting humor into your meetings. No, not pie-in-the-face slapstick, the ministry of silly walks, or (potentially) offensive jokes.

The authors used their own flavor of humor throughout the book, which, while some would call it corny dad humor, we find quite hilarious. In fact, we're laughing right now as we write this. Really. But that's just us! Like all dads, we think we're a laugh riot even while others are rolling their eyes.

When we met with each other for this book, we kept it light. We started with trivia questions, occasionally told bad dad jokes. It may have taken a while, but then we always got down to business. We know this because right now instead of reading a book chock full of wisdom about meetings, you instead would be reading a book entirely filed with blank pages. Perhaps such a book full of blank pages could come in handy to take notes at bad meetings—which they would be, as you'd be without that wisdom. But isn't it better to have to bring a notepad to record all of the insanely innovative and actionable ideas your team has produced because the meeting was planned and facilitated so well by you after reading the nonblank book?

Now in addition to all the (hopefully) good stuff we told you about meetings, we also stressed the importance of team building. Remember, the name of this book is: *Great Meetings Build Great Teams: A Guide for Project Leaders and Agilists*.

No, as we stated earlier, we're not naïve enough to think that great meetings will build successful teams all by themselves. But certainly, consistently lousy meetings will undermine your team and will not help morale.

To bring it full circle, we would like to remind you of what Peter Taylor said in the foreword—"We settled on a tagline for our group which is 'Together Everyone Achieves More' (TEAM), and we truly believe this to be true." So do we.

We trust that the book indeed does have more value than a blank set of bound pages. We share our experiences with you for that purpose and wish you successful meetings and thus—successful projects!

Meeting Rules of the Road (Suitable for Framing)

- Good meeting preparation is a must. You can't execute a good meeting if you haven't planned for it. And when you prepare, put yourself in the shoes of various attendees.
- Be large and in charge. People are looking for authority, for a leader, whether it's for a 15-minute meeting or a one-week class.
- If you can't take charge of a meeting, people (maybe even your sponsor) will wonder if you can lead a project.
- Do not let people hijack your meeting.
- Timekeeping during a meeting is crucial. The next thing you know, 25 minutes will go by with nothing accomplished. Feel free to yell out "15 minutes left!" It's useful and creates a sense of urgency and reinforces the idea that you are leading the meeting (and the project).
- Be aware of people's body language. It will tell you a lot. It's more challenging virtually but not impossible. People's faces say a lot. Humans are never not communicating!
- Be culturally aware—whether that culture is organizational, or regional/national. When in Rome, do as the Romans do. When in Schenectady, do as the Schenectadians do.
- Use meetings as a golden opportunity to build that project team. Understand team formation dynamics. You can use the meeting itself to build the team or do fun stuff like escape rooms, outward bound, or even a trip to the bowling alley or sporting event.
- Ask yourself the following question—"Is this meeting even necessary?"

- Have an agenda.
- Frame agenda items as questions (if you cannot frame them as questions, maybe you don't really need the meeting). This will help you create actionable meeting results.
- Facilitate, facilitate, facilitate. Get that meeting moving. Make it happen. If you don't know how, hire an outsider. Your team can (and should be) the SMEs.
- Plan your meeting out well in advance and think of everything that could go wrong. And then have a contingency in case something *does* go wrong. And give everyone your cell phone number so that they can contact you.
- Virtual meetings are a different beast—it's unnatural. Understand the differences! Watch out for Zoom fatigue. Keep meetings brief. Have tools and know how to use them.
- Stakeholders, stakeholders, stakeholders. Ignore them at your peril.
- Use icebreakers to allow people to get to know each other in a fun way. Don't forget to have fun once in a while.
- Follow-up on the meeting action items. If you have no name and no date next to the action items, then precisely nobody will work on them, forever.
- Be sure to use humor in your meetings. Not to the point where someone says "What do you mean I'm funny? Funny *how*? Like I'm a *clown*, I *amuse* you?" (With apologies to Martin Scorsese and *Goodfellas*.)

Glossary

Agile/Adaptive. A change-driven approach to managing projects that grew out of software development. It's iterative and adaptive, creating deliverables in short (up to one month) iterations or sprints. Self-organizing teams work closely with product owners to continually create business value. (Compare with waterfall.) Variants include Scrum, XP, and Lean.

Assumption. For the purposes of project management (and in particular for this book, which is focused on meetings), think of an assumption as the seed of a risk. If you assume, for example, that the price of a key material for your project is steady, and that price triples, then that assumption has germinated and started to grow into a threat. The formal definition of an assumption is something considered to be true without any proof. From a meeting perspective, what's important is to make these assumptions widely known and documented—and to consider them when you're identifying risks.

Baseline. A baseline is a reference, based on original project starting conditions, against which all measurements will be compared. Baselines are approved by key stakeholders. Three baselines—schedule, cost, and scope—are used in project management to look for variance and make changes. The baseline can be changed but only with formal change control (waterfall only).

Communications plan. A plan that details how communications will flow within the team and all other stakeholders. For example, there will be a weekly team meeting to discuss action items, schedule, and risks. There will be a monthly steering committee meeting to advise senior management of progress. There will be a lessons learned meeting at the end of each phase to determine what can be done better.

Constraint. A limit that cannot be exceeded. In the case of projects, we're normally talking about budget, schedule, and scope. See *Triple constraint*.

Crashing. A form of schedule compression in which extra resources are put on critical-path tasks to get those specific tasks done more quickly. This can potentially bring the project's end date in earlier than indicated by a natural determination of the critical path. It may result in increased risk and/or cost. Adding too many people may lead to the law of diminishing returns (waterfall only).

Critical path. In a network diagram, this is the longest path through the network, which, in turn, defines the shortest time possible in which the project could be completed without applying techniques such as fast-tracking or crashing. A critical-path task will have no slack (float), which means that if it slips, even by one second, that one-second delay will cause the same delay in the end date. There may be more than one critical path in a network. See *Network diagram* (waterfall only).

Critical success factors (CSFs). When creating CSFs, remember that they always relate to objectives. Figure B.1 shows how our case study may develop CSFs from its objectives.

Objective	CSF	Success criteria
Gain 25% more of the electorate with the environment as a top concern.	Assemble compelling information about the sustainability elements of this home.	90 percent of appropriate statistics compiled within 2 months of launch
	Assure that the information is conveyed to the target voters.	50 percent increase in website hits 75 percent positive reaction on social media.
Maintain a Think Globally, Act Locally way of working in the project.	Use high-profile vendors such as Tesla Roofing, but insist on hiring staff from the Escondido area.	95 percent of all workers are from within a 25-mile radius.
Assure that selected vendors are ethical and responsible.	Use intern staff to vet vendors.	100 percent of vendors vetted.

Objective	CSF	Success criteria
	Review lessons learned from similar sustainable housing projects.	At least two other similar projects are used for lessons learned.
	Involve vendor stakeholders early in the project to assure their buy-in to objectives and working principles.	85 percent attendance rate for key identified stakeholders at kickoff.
Achieve and document 45 percent energy reduction after 2 years.	Baseline current energy use.	Baseline complete by March 30, 2019.
	Assure that utility service providers are recording ongoing energy use.	100% of providers have committed by July 15, 2019.
	Use intern staff to collect, compare, and report data each month for the 24-month period.	Benchmark: Achieve 30% savings within first year.
	Acquire LEED expert for consultation	N/A

Figure B.1 Develop CSFs from objectives

Definition of Done. In Agile, an agreed-upon list of the activities considered necessary to move a product increment, usually represented by a user story, to a done state by the end of a sprint.

Dependency. A dependency is a relationship between tasks in which one must be completed before the other. They are represented by arrows in a network diagram. In our case study, we cannot put on the candles, for example, until the two dependencies (obtain candles and frost and decorate cake) are completed (waterfall only).

Estimate. A forecast regarding how long an activity will take, how many resources might be required, or how much it will cost.

Facilitate. To make it possible or easier for something to happen. For our purposes, it means to lead or guide a meeting to successful conclusion.

Fast-tracking. A form of schedule compression in which you do tasks in parallel that are usually, for best practice reasons, done in sequence (e.g., making sure that a design is complete before beginning construction). This tends to increase risk and may also increase costs (waterfall only).

Float. The amount of time that a task can slip without delaying the project's end date (also known as slack) (waterfall only).

Gantt chart. The Gantt chart is named in honor of Henry Gantt, an American mechanical engineer and management consultant known for the development of scientific management. It's a visual representation of the WBS with the element of time and a calendar added. The Gantt chart uses bars to represent when the tasks start and end, arrows to represent dependencies, and diamonds to represent milestones. It may also track resource usage, percent compete, and other attributes. Figure B.2 shows a simple example using our bake-a-cake saga described in our glossary entry for *network diagram.* (Tends to be used mostly in waterfall. Agile uses a higher-level roadmap.)

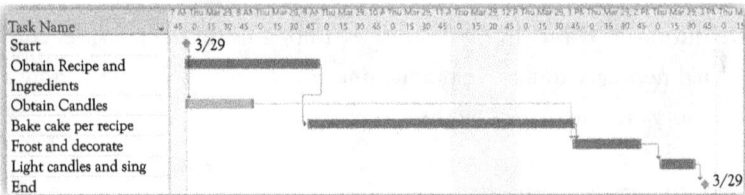

Figure B.2 Sample Gantt chart (Microsoft project)

Issue log. Similar to a risk register but dedicated instead to issues – threats that have already been triggered or are currently occurring. Issue logs are in place to assure that issues have owners and dates for resolution and are tracked *to* that resolution. Issue logs provide accountability.

Kanban board (task board.) An agile project management tool designed to help visualize work, limit work-in-progress, and maximize efficiency (or flow).

Milestone. An important project moment usually representing a key project accomplishment or due date, such as End of 3rd Quarter or Complete Audit or Field Test Complete. Milestones have zero duration by definition and are represented as diamonds on network diagrams and Gantt charts.

Network diagram. A means of displaying the project schedule in terms of project tasks, their durations, and interdependencies. If, for example, you need to know how long it will take to prepare a homemade birthday cake for a party, you need to get ingredients, bake the cake, frost the cake, and decorate the cake. In parallel you could buy candles. Arrows show dependencies and the amount of slack (float) available for each task. It can also indicate any lag times (such as baking time) and lead time (like allowing a task to have a head start).

The network diagram is best for graphically showing the critical path of the project—the sequence of tasks in which a delay of any of them will cause the project to fail to meet its planned end-date. In our highly simplified example, if Obtain Candles turns out to be eight hours, it will make the path Obtain Candles–Put on Candles–Light Candles–Sing the longest path (critical path) through the network. (Waterfall only)

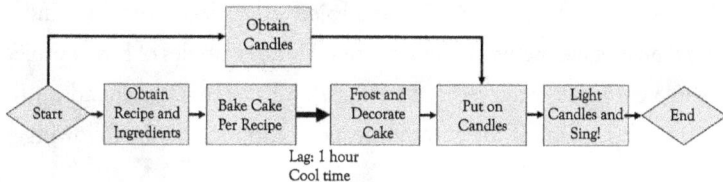

Figure B.3 Critical path for baking a cake

Project charter. The fundamental document that authorizes a project and names the project manager. It's meant to be a terse, concise document that summarizes the objectives, stakeholders, high-level budget, assumptions, and risks.

RACI matrix. This is one form of a responsibility assignment matrix, and it maps the what (the tasks of the project) to the who (the contributors to the project). RACI stands for responsible, accountable, consulted, and informed, and (see Figure 9.1) at the intersection of the *what* and the *who* it defines just what the contributor contributes.

Requirement. A capability needed in a product, service, application, or result that satisfies a need—solving a problem or achieving an objective of a stakeholder. Typically, requirements for projects are from customers or the project team itself. An example of a customer requirement: the software must be able to provide its result on a PC, tablet, or smartphone screen. An example of a project requirement: project team meetings must have an agenda.

Risk register. A list of the risks on the project, including both threats (negative risks) and opportunities (positive risks), that captures the risk, risk type, risk owner, planned risk response, possible secondary or residual risks, and more. From a meeting perspective, this is important, because risk should be a conscious agenda item at every other project meeting, at a minimum.

Scrum. A framework within which people can address complex adaptive problems while productively and creatively delivering products of the highest possible value.

Schedule. Although it may be displayed in many forms, the schedule serves to show how activities in the project take place over time and as well as the linkages between the activities. Some examples of how a project schedule could be conveyed at meetings (and in general) depend on the audience and intent of the communication, and include the following:

- Using a regular calendar with key project milestones highlighted
- A milestone chart or summary table of key milestone events
- A Gantt chart
- A network diagram (with or without timeline)

In all of the cases, the schedule is focused on the when of the project. It's important to note that the scope is determined first, or the schedule won't reflect the full set of project activities and may be missing key dependencies.

Scope. What is *in* and *not in* a project. Scope must not only be clearly defined but must be carefully controlled. Otherwise, the project may incrementally and dangerously expand, leading to increased costs and delayed schedule. After all, scope is one side of the classic triple constraint of project management. The main component of scope is the work focused on the project's outcome.

However, it's important to understand that this has two components—*project scope* and *product scope*. Project scope is the work performed on behalf of the delivery of the project's product, service, or result. For example, if we're building a home, and we discover that having nourishing snacks for the construction workers makes a significant difference in their productivity, we may choose to provide those snacks.

The snacks themselves are not delivered to the homeowners, but they are important and are a part of *project* scope. Product scope, in this example, would include the home itself as well as landscaping, installation of appliances, whatever was defined as the final deliverable(s), and delivered to customers.

Sprint. A time-boxed iteration of a product or project development cycle. It contains a planned amount of work that a development team chooses to complete work to demonstrate to product owner and stakeholders.

Stakeholder. A person or organization that is affected by your project or the project's outcome. If you're building a bridge, the stakeholders would be the construction workers, the project team members, the suppliers of materials, the pedestrians and drivers who use the bridge, the businesses whose sales may change based on changed traffic patterns . . . as you can see, a stakeholder has a broad definition. It's imperative that you do a broad and deep identification of stakeholders because stakeholders bring with them their own set of risks—both threats and opportunities. The project manager has to balance the competing objectives of stakeholders.

Triple constraint. This is a way to think of the three most important and interdependent constraints that all projects face—time (schedule), cost (budget), and scope (what's in and not in the project). Typically, you cannot change one of the constraints without affecting either one or both of the other constraints. Be sure that your project team is aware not only of this concept but also of the priority of each of these in your particular project. Make that prioritization a recurring theme at your meetings.

User story. Short, simple descriptions of a feature told from the perspective of the person who desires the new capability, usually a user or customer of the system.

Waterfall. A methodology that defines the project life cycle as a series of phases that must be completed before moving on to the next one (see Figure B.4). Phases can be run in an overlapping or parallel fashion at the expense of some risk. Waterfall tends to be very plan driven. See *agile/adaptive*.

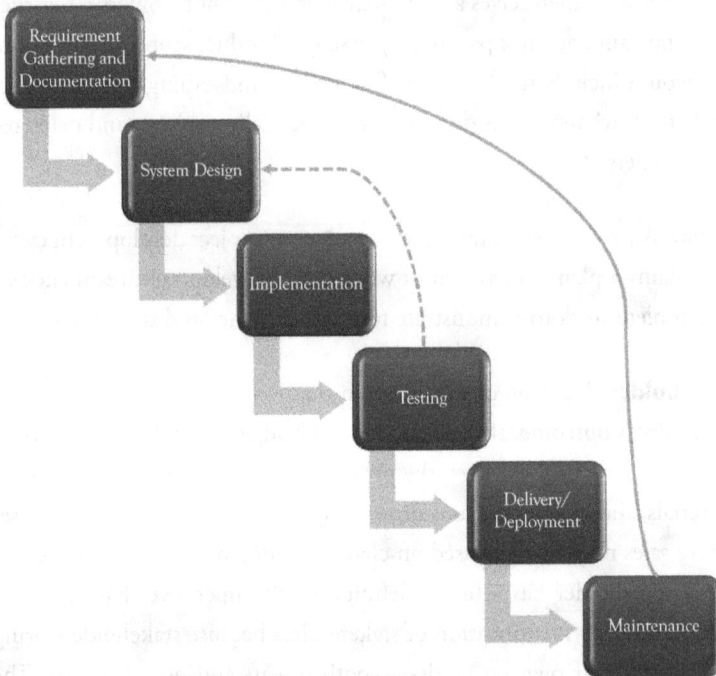

Figure B.4 Example of waterfall methodology

Work breakdown structure (WBS). A hierarchical structure to visualize the scope of a project. Think of it as an organization chart for your project. It's important to remember that the WBS depicts everything that's in your project, including both product scope (the features and deliverables of your product) and project scope (aspects needed to deliver that product scope).

The WBS's lower levels will show work packages that can be assigned to individual groups or organizations and can also be used for accounting purposes (charging hours), and that will form the basis of the tasks on the Gantt chart. The sum of all of the elements in the WBS must represent *everything* that's needed to deliver the project's outcome (which will be at the very top of the WBS). A partial WBS is shown in Figure B.5 to give you the idea. Foundation, Frame, and so on would be broken down similar to the way that Electrical and Solar Roof are as shown in the illustration (waterfall only).

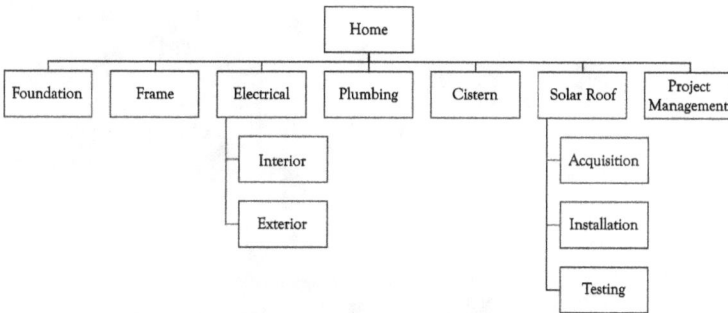

Figure B.5 Sample WBS for building a sustainable house

About the Authors

Rich Maltzman, PMP, has coauthored several books on project leadership, including *Bridging the PM Competency Gap*, and the Cleland-award winning *Green Project Management*. He teaches a suite of courses in project leadership, serving as a Master Lecturer at Boston University.

Jim Stewart, PMP, has facilitated dozens of project meetings, from kickoffs to planning meetings to Scrum events. As an independent project consultant and Agile coach, he advises on best practices, teaches project management, and strategizes and executes on Agile transformations.

Index

OTHER TITLES IN THE PORTFOLIO AND PROJECT MANAGEMENT COLLECTION

Timothy J. Kloppenborg, Xavier University and
Kam Jugdev, Athabasca University, Editors

- *When Graduation's Over, Learning Begins* by Roger Forsgren
- *Project Control Methods and Best Practices* by Yakubu Olawale
- *Managing Projects With PMBOK 7* by James W. Marion and Tracey Richardson
- *Shields Up* by Gregory J. Skulmoski
- *Greatness in Construction History* by Sherif Hashem
- *The Inner Building Blocks* by Abhishek Rai
- *Project Profitability* by Reginald Tomas Lee
- *Moving the Needle With Lean OKRs* by Bart den Haak
- *Lean Knowledge Management* by Roger Forsgren
- *The MBA Distilled for Project & Program Professionals* by Bradley D. Clark
- *Project Management for Banks* by Dan Bonner
- *Successfully Achieving Strategy Through Effective Portfolio Management* by Frank R. Parth

Concise and Applied Business Books

The Collection listed above is one of 30 business subject collections that Business Expert Press has grown to make BEP a premiere publisher of print and digital books. Our concise and applied books are for...

- Professionals and Practitioners
- Faculty who adopt our books for courses
- Librarians who know that BEP's Digital Libraries are a unique way to offer students ebooks to download, not restricted with any digital rights management
- Executive Training Course Leaders
- Business Seminar Organizers

Business Expert Press books are for anyone who needs to dig deeper on business ideas, goals, and solutions to everyday problems. Whether one print book, one ebook, or buying a digital library of 110 ebooks, we remain the affordable and smart way to be business smart. For more information, please visit www.businessexpertpress.com, or contact sales@businessexpertpress.com.

www.ingramcontent.com/pod-product-compliance
Lightning Source LLC
Chambersburg PA
CBHW061212220326
41599CB00025B/4612